"THEY STILL

"THEY STILL PICK ME UP WHEN I FALL"

THE ROLE OF CARING IN
YOUTH DEVELOPMENT AND COMMUNITY LIFE

Diana Mendley Rauner

COLUMBIA UNIVERSITY PRESS   NEW YORK

Columbia University Press

Publishers Since 1893

New York   Chichester, West Sussex

Copyright © 2000 Diana Mendley Rauner

Rauner, Diana Mendley.
    They still pick me up when I fall: the role of caring in youth devel-
opment and community life / Diana Mendley Rauner.
        p. cm.
    Includes bibliographical references and index.
    ISBN 0–231–11854–6 (cl)—ISBN 0-231-11855-4 (pa)
        1. Social work with youth—United States. 2. Social work with
youth—United States—Case studies. I. Title.

HV1431 .R38 2000
362.7'083—dc21   00–026739

Printed in the United States of America
c 10 9 8 7 6 5 4 3 2 1
p 10 9 8 7 6 5 4 3 2 1

To my parents,
Laura and Mark Mendley

CONTENTS

ACKNOWLEDGMENTS

If a book can be said to have godparents, this one claims two: Joan Lipsitz and Harold Richman. Joan planted the seeds of this work with her vision of a field of caring, and Harold fostered it through his support and guidance of difficult conceptual work.

While at the Lilly Endowment, Joan Lipsitz initiated the research inquiry into youth and caring that began to map a field for others, including myself, to follow. Through their support Joan and Willis Bright of the Endowment have nurtured the field of caring for over ten years. The Lilly Endowment provided the financial support for the research and writing of this book, as well as encouragement and practical input from staff with broad-ranging experience with youth programs. The Endowment also provided me with a cabal of advisers, including Peter Benson, Joyce Epstein, Norman Newberg, Michael Resnick, Joan Schine, Janie Ward, and Emmy Werner, whose wisdom and attentiveness were invaluable.

This book exists because Harold Richman and others at Chapin Hall Center for Children have ceaselessly promoted the importance of understanding what works in supporting healthy children, families, and communities. Harold championed this effort, offering guidance, support, and an unflagging committment to the ideas and purpose of this work. Rob Chaskin set forth many of the initial thoughts on which my ideas are built. Many other colleagues at Chapin Hall have contributed to this work, especially Anne Clary, Susan Campbell, Joan Costello, Rebecca Stone, and Joan Wynn. Beth Browning, Kent Burbank, and Rachel Stevens provided intelligent and exhaustive research support. Amanda Toler retyped countless drafts.

This book would not have been possible without the efforts and trust of the six caring organizations profiled here. Each allowed me unfettered access, letting me trail along on camping trips, pizza breaks, and farm chores, and took the time to ensure that I truly understood what was special about their programs. The staff of these organizations unselfconsciously shared their wisdom and experience and made it possible for the youths in their care to speak openly and in their own voices.

As always, my most profound thanks go to my family: to my husband, Bruce Rauner, whose essential comfort, sense of humor and uncommon sense sustain me; to my parents, Laura and Mark Mendley, whose habits of care have been my most important education in community; and to Genara Gonzalez, who provided exceptional, loving care to my three small children during many of the hours I devoted to this book.

"*They Still Pick Me Up When I Fall*"

CHAPTER 1

CARING FOR OUR YOUTH: A CALL TO ACTION

Lydia,* a senior at El Puente Academy for Peace and Justice in Brooklyn, New York, was kicked out of her previous school. At El Puente, she is a straight-A student with hopes of attending Columbia University to study science. She attributes much of her success to her school's principal, Frances Lucerna. "Babies . . . need people to help them learn to walk and help them up when they fall . . . I'm big and I'm not a baby but they still pick me up when I fall . . . Frances always has her hands out grabbing onto anybody who falls to pick them right up again" and here Lydia cups her hands together and moves them from place to place like a safety net.

This book is a call to action to anyone who works for and worries about the next generation. It is about how we care for those who are "big"—youths who no longer need the care given to babies and children, but who still need support and guidance. It is an attempt to set out the terms of a dialogue about what it means to care for young people at all levels of social interaction: as individuals, in a professional capacity, within an organization, and as a society. It is meant to help us come to some consensus about what we want for young people, and what needs to be done to provide it. The focus is on caring as an organizing concept—despite objections that it is trite or overused—because caring is the essential component of influential relationships.

Caring has not been the currency of debate about young people for some time. Talk about youth tends to focus on stricter inputs, such as uniforms,

---

*All of the young people quoted in this book are identified with aliases.

mandatory service, and adult criminal sentencing—and on measurable outcomes: standardized tests, job prospects, and drug testing. There has been little room in national dialogue for what kind of people we want our youths to become, for the important outcomes for them as human beings and for our society as a plural democracy. We need to rethink these questions in terms that allow us to articulate the importance of community, citizenship, social justice, and morality without resorting to platitudes. *"They Still Pick Me Up When I Fall"* attempts to craft new language for addressing these essential questions.

This book is also meant to integrate the theories and concepts of research and philosophy with the practical concerns of those who work with youth. So many teachers and youth workers know, intuitively, why it is important that youth develop in a context filled with care; but they may lack access to the concepts that will give their knowledge power and meaning. An intellectual context can improve practice by giving youth workers a broader framework in which to see their efforts and a deeper understanding of the processes involved in youth development. Likewise, the work of researchers needs the grounding available only through the experience of practice. Connecting these two worlds might improve both.

There have been many essays on the dire status of youth, citing alarming statistics that show fewer supports and greater stresses in many young people's lives. Yet there is also a discernible yearning among many adults to reconnect, to make a difference, to help. People gather and march, or meet and weep, but often do not know how to translate their sentiments into tangible actions. Many do not know how to begin actively caring for that which they care about. Those that do take small actions are often frustrated as to the larger impact of their efforts.

This book is an attempt to mobilize this energy into intentional actions that make sense both in individual contexts and in the context of broad social and political change. There is much confusion over how care for young people should be expressed, by whom, and through what structures and institutions. We know that care for the young is essential, but in our competitive society we are not able to find the means to support the care of many. Likewise, people wish to express connectivity and caring, but often feel they lack the organizations and structures through which to act. We recognize that these issues are important, and yet we do not even have the words to begin discussing how to address them.

Over time, caring has been relegated to a special set of relationships and institutions. We have come to see caring as a powerless civility, a feature of face-to-face interactions defined and experienced by individuals. We are more comfortable talking about a caring teacher than a caring community or a caring society. We have tended to see schools and other important institutions as value-neutral product providers with no caregiving role or responsibility. But it can be enlightening to analyze the activities of individuals, institutions, and large-scale social systems as providers of care. Viewing care as a quality of social structures allows us to find the interconnections between caring in interpersonal relationships and caring experienced through the collective associations and institutions in which we all participate. When the terrain of caring is defined so broadly, it is not enough to counsel kindness in face-to-face encounters. We must also think, quite radically, about how we can organize the social, civic, and economic institutions in which we participate so that they are caring places as well.

We can think of caring as occurring in a four-tiered hierarchy of increasing complexity. Most of us identify care with the most basic of these tiers: spontaneous, individual face-to-face interactions between strangers, friends, or kin. But care is also practiced in other domains. The actions of professionals with their charges—teachers, youth workers, service providers, and supervisors—can be infused with caring if these professionals adopt caring behaviors. In doing so they are caring as individuals in their professional roles. Likewise, organizations can be caring by consciously arranging their practices, programs, and policies along an ethic of care. Individuals in their professional capacity perform caring actions, but the organization, by virtue of its structure and functioning, also can facilitate and promote effective caring behavior. Finally, a society can be caring by adopting policies that support interdependence, promote the well-being of those most in need, and favor caring organizations. Of course, it is individuals who shape policy, write laws, and elect representatives; but those individuals are acting in their public capacity, and their actions are mediated through a large and institutionalized social system. This system, in turn, affects individuals through its impact on organizations, both public and private.

Thinking of ourselves as caregivers with many possible roles in a system of care can help organize and give meaning to our actions. There are many levels at which we can translate our concerns into actions, and many vehicles for expressing care. But to feel part of a larger effort and mobilize others towards it, we must first recognize it as such. We must understand ourselves as engaged in a common endeavor to care for the next generation. We must describe this work as effected by various institutions of our society as well as by individuals. We must name our vision.

FINDING WORDS

> Human existence cannot be silent, nor can it
> be nourished by false words, but only by true
> words, with which men transform the world.
> To exist, humanly, is to *name* the world, to
> change it."
> —Paolo Freire, *Pedagogy of the Oppressed.*[1]

It is in the process of applying words to experiences that we begin to make sense of them. By naming a condition, as Freire says, we take the first step towards recognizing it as a discrete entity and understanding how it acts upon our lives. Having words to explain phenomena, concepts, and objects of importance is largely how we are able to grasp the phenomena themselves. As abstract signifiers of often complex, rich concepts, words allow those that use them to act consciously, deliberately, and in coordination with others. The words we use to explain our world are important.

Caring is a word of great power with a long, rich, and sometimes tired past. Its power comes from its broad accessibility to social actors, as well as from the depth and complexity of the concepts with which it is associated. Yet the word has often been trivialized, and thus marginalized, in the important business of considering interpersonal relationships and larger systems of social interaction. Like its counterparts, love and hope, caring is all too often used as a sugarcoated word, encountered on a greeting card. After so much overexposure, the very concept of caring might seem trite or meaningless.

The power of caring as a word rests in its history in our philosophical, religious, and cultural traditions. It is tempting to replace "caring" with a technical term that evokes the many connotations of caring that are important for study and research. But unlike technical terms familiar only to experts, care is accessible to everyone. What is so valuable about the word "caring" is its folk usage, its cultural associations. But because caring means something different to everyone, it has had limited utility in discussions of the practices, ideals, and motivations of interpersonal and social responsibilities.

"They Still Pick Me Up When I Fall" is motivated by the conviction that many important aspects of caring have been overlooked and underexamined. It assumes that care is a powerful concept referring to values and motivations often absent from current public dialogue, in particular dialogue about the positive development of children and young people. Rather than create a new word to replace caring, this book will seek to clarify a useful conceptualization

of this common word. The following chapters address this task through two disparate means. Part of the task of reexamining caring is to understand the assumptions that situate its meaning in the context of our culture and our social practices. This effort demands that we consider the structure of our institutions, the rituals by which we express our understanding of the life cycle, and the ways by which we express our shared values and myths. In examining caring in this manner, we are really considering the ways in which caring is valued and demonstrated in our culture.

Some of the best information about the meaning of care in our society comes from the adults and youths who work at care and think about its role in practical terms. An equally important aspect of the effort to redefine care involves capturing the values and methods of exemplary care providers. This task requires not only reporting on successful schools and youth programs, but seeking to distill the essential processes that comprise caring work. In such a way will we "re-name" caring.

Throughout the book research and philosophy offering an intellectual framework for care is woven with the voices of the youth workers and young people for whom caring is made real in scores of small interactions and large decisions. The following chapters intertwine conceptual thinking and research findings with the stories of six practically focused efforts to use caring behaviors to support the development of young people into responsible, productive members of society. These programs have been chosen to illustrate the broad range of activities that can have care as their focus and the diverse youths who need and benefit from care relationships. Though very different from each other, all of these exemplary programs are motivated by a perspective that sees caring as the fundamental purpose and underlying principle of youth work:

• In Gallup, New Mexico, young people are engaged in rock climbing, search and rescue teams, and other outdoor adventure activities in a successful substance abuse prevention program run by the National Indian Youth Leadership Project. Drawing on traditional themes and customs, the programs offer Native American youths constructive activities and the opportunity to reconnect with their community and cultural values.

• In suburban Chicago, young people gather at The Warming House, a drop-in counseling center that serves as a haven, social center, and "home away from home" for high school students in the community. Young staff members are on hand to maintain safety and protection, talk through a young person's problems, or just play a game of pool.

• In Kansas City, Missouri, young men ages 16 to 19 serve as "Block Brothers"—mentors, big brothers, friends, and role models—for fifteen or more young people in their immediate neighborhood. Sponsored by the local chapter of the Boys and Girls Club, this program seeks to develop habits of leadership and service in older adolescents as well as to provide care and enrichment to children ages 6 through 14.[2]

• In Brooklyn, New York, high school students at El Puente Academy of Peace and Justice explore a curriculum organized around themes of peace, justice, love, and caring that extends from the classroom into the streets of their working-class Latino community. At this school within a community center, the school day blends into afterschool and civic activities as teachers, staff, and young people alike work together on projects to serve the community.

• In rural Vermont, high school students learn cooperation, responsibility, and habits of care and respect along with agricultural and land conservation skills at Smokey House Center. Working in teams of six alongside adult crew leaders, young people experience a work environment that both demands high standards and offers support and guidelines for behavior.

• IIn Gary, Indiana, young people affiliated with the Tree of Life Ministry teach, mentor, and counsel their peers and younger children in a comprehensive community revitalization project organized around economic self-sufficiency, family support, and spiritual awakening. In this large evangelical ministry, young people are active, contributing members of a community of worshipers that has taken on the social and economic challenges of inner-city Gary as its mission.

These six programs reflect the wide range of venues and structures that offer organized care to young people. Throughout the book, they will serve as windows into caring practices, touchstones that make real the sometimes abstract concepts that surround care. These programs are intended to show how program design, organizing philosophies, and interactions among staff and between staff and young people are all infused with values of care. They are offered not as templates, but as examples of care in practice that might be useful to those who work with youths, their teachers, and parents who wish to understand more about how organizations can care for youth.

These exemplars are also meant to demonstrate how youth work is, fundamentally, all about care. Regardless of the activity or venue, all of these programs and others like them are doing the same thing—building caring relationships between youths and between youths and adults. They are vehicles for caring. Their primary purpose is to engage young people in relationships in which they have the opportunity to learn and practice the skills of successful interaction that will allow them to function as healthy adults. Despite the differences in orientation of teachers, youth workers, counselors, and youth service employers, they are united in this common goal.

To say that youth work is all about caring is only helpful if the activity can be clarified with specific language. Staying in the realm of the practical, there are specific actions and behaviors that effect care. This is care as an active process, not a sentiment or an attitude alone. Care can be modeled as a process involving three components—-attentiveness, responsiveness, and competence—that operate interactively. Attentiveness involves actively seeking awareness of others and their needs and points of view. Responsiveness refers to the motivation to extend oneself on behalf of others. Competence, one's ability to do something about another's needs, refers to the essentially practical nature of this model of care. It is not enough merely to have good intentions; for caring to matter it must be effective as well. This model will be more fully discussed in the next chapter, and will serve as a framework for understanding the ways in which young people are cared for in organized settings and the skills we must try to help youths develop.

With a model of care in hand, we can also consider how the practice of care transcends the emotions and behavior of individuals. We wish to understand how the actions of individuals can aggregate to create a caring organization, a caring community, and a caring society. These components of care offer a means by which to describe organizations as more or less attentive, responsive, or competent. They allow us to talk about the connections between practicing attentiveness in face-to-face interactions and in one's role as a citizen, between individual responsiveness and the responsiveness of a group, organization, or society. And they offer a way of holding institutions to the same standards of care that we expect of individuals.

A workable definition in terms that are meaningful to its users is essential to broad acceptance of a word. In this case, the users of "caring" are likely to be almost everyone: parents, teachers, policy makers—everyone with a stake in supporting the positive development and socialization of the next generation. Historically, these groups have not approached these concerns with a common language. An aim of this book is to demonstrate that caring is a useful term that permits social actors, researchers, educators, and others to speak the same language about some core concepts that affect children's development and social conditions.

A discussion of caring must include empirical evidence about the role of caring in positive youth development. At this point, many of the connections implied in a fully realized conceptualization of caring are a priori, morally and logically generated ideas for which little empirical evidence has been amassed. A clearly conceptualized definition of caring can provide a framework for future empirical research.

With a clearly articulated common understanding of the word and concrete examples of its practice, we can begin a dialogue about the role and meaning of care in our society. Such a dialogue, in Freire's words, "the encounter of men addressed to the common task of learning and acting," can be a means by which we work to improve the care of our children and youth. It is hoped that this book will inspire dialogue and reflection among individuals, as well as within organizations and communities. The model of attentiveness, responsiveness, and competence can be a useful framework for self-evaluation, as well as for families, schools, religious institutions, and other organizations seeking to understand how to care more effectively for youth. This book can also be used to hold a mirror up to ourselves, and to begin a real dialogue about caring by describing what we see.

A dialogue about caring for children and youth can take many forms. It might involve renewed attention to the key roles that relationships play in both individual development and the success of group endeavors. It could include a reexamination of the practices by which caring adults build relationships with youth. It could involve a discussion of the structure and purpose of institutions through which some care is provided. And it could lead to greater exploration of the ways in which the policies and practices of our society do or do not support young people and their development into caring citizens.

If done thoroughly, however, a reexamination of caring is likely to be a subversive exercise. Caring is as much a political philosophy as a guide to face-to-face interaction. It recognizes no boundaries between the values we espouse in our family and those that guide our actions in the public sphere. The same ethic practiced in face-to-face interactions becomes a template for social norms. One cannot dig too deeply into our culture's values without confronting conflicts between caring values and the self-focused, competitive attitudes that dominate much of modern culture. It is illogical to talk of caring environments for young people in the larger context of an unquestioned social system. If we probe deeply into caring, we are likely to challenge many of the assumptions on which our society rests.

AN ETHIC OF CARE

Today in our culture, care for children is seen as an exclusively private activity, and increasingly an activity of the nuclear family alone. Modern, Western societies have focused an unprecedented degree of responsibility on the nuclear family as the almost sole provider of direct care for children and youth. However, in recent decades, the nuclear family has increasingly been in jeopardy, suffering under the stress of more family hours devoted to work outside the home, rising rates of divorce and single parenthood, and high geographic mobility. It is, perhaps, not too much to say that our society has a large, collective "parental care deficit."

But parental care has never been the only means of caring for children. In all societies throughout history, families have joined together to share in the collective work of raising children and to offer support and stability to individuals. These associations can be called tribes, neighborhoods, or communities; they can be formed around places of worship or economic activity; and they can be organized as schools, voluntary associations, or religious institutions. They are distinguished by the voluntary participation of their members; that participation is, ideally, sustained by a shared set of values. The sociologist Peter Berger called these institutions *mediating structures*[4]; the care they provide to children and their families can be called *organized, facilitated care*. Whether provided by neighbors, teachers, or professional youth workers, whether occurring in a local playlot or in a church basement, organized care has always been a part of children's lives. In some cases, its presence has served mainly as a social support for families. However, at some points in many young people's lives, the relationships and experiences available through organized care offer important developmental opportunities that parents alone cannot provide.

Organized, facilitated care does not replace parental care, and a strong network of organized care providers does not diminish the importance of the family. Yet, while parental care is unquestionably foundational and, in most cases, primary throughout childhood and adolescence, as children grow it is more and more necessary to complement the care offered at home with experiences in the larger world that support and sustain parents' values and aspirations for their children. Organized care is meant to be complementary, not competitive, with family values and organization. This is why, ideally, such care arises from citizens rather than being imposed by government. It is part of the spontaneous, voluntary associations that comprise community.

As the stresses of family life have limited parents' abilities to invest time in their children, they have likewise caused these voluntary associations to suffer. This disinvestment has grave consequences, for it is in these associations that social trust and community reside. Without the connections created by personal investment in relationships, the world outside the family becomes one of contractual exchanges and carefully proscribed rights. The relationships that comprise community depend on the active involvement of a large portion of the citizenry. They cannot be privatized or contracted out.

Disinvestment in communal care for children and youth is particularly pernicious, because development and socialization of the young is essential to the maintenance of society. All members of a community share an interest in and a responsibility for the development of the next generation. In its most functional, basic sense, care is the means by which young people are prepared to assume the adult roles and responsibilities required by their culture. This process is of enormous value to the entire community, because without a next generation of productive, socialized adults, the society cannot sustain itself. There is no society in history that has not recognized the necessity of providing its children the physical, emotional, social, and economic means to become productive and sustaining members of their community.

Alongside the imperative for shared commitment to youth stands an equally critical need to instill in young people an awareness of the connections between their private and public morality. Young people need to understand the relevance of their values as individuals in face-to-face interactions to their roles as professionals, members of organizations, and citizens. We must articulate expectations for them that focus not only on their private morality and public achievements but also on their role in creating and sustaining community. Just as we concern ourselves with the means by which we socialize our youth, we must ask ourselves to what we are socializing them. How can we demonstrate the importance of care and social responsibility alongside individually focused measures of success and punitive responses to failure?

This is a moral argument. Advocating communal responsibility for the care of the next generation implies an ethic of care that crosses the realms of morality, culture, and reason, and respects no division between the private and the public. A worldview organized around care argues for an ethic that stands beside, and reinforces, the work ethic and ethic of individual responsibility that are dominant in our culture. It is the vision of a life organized around commitments and shared responsibilities in which interdependence, mutuality, and nurturance are seen as public, as well as private, virtues. In this perspective, care is not solely the provenance of the private sphere, but rather a critical and pervasive force throughout society. This is caring as a social norm.

A vision of a society in which the development of the next generation is valued as a public good, in which interdependence and mutuality are celebrated in public life as well as private, in which care is held as an essential guiding ethic for all social relations seems hopelessly idealistic. But is it? Can we envision a world in which caring for people, ideas, and projects is truly the point of life? Where our doctrines and institutions, as well as the structure and organization of everyday life, reflect values of common effort, trustworthiness, and cooperation? If such a world is possible, what does it take to create it?

BEGINNING THE INQUIRY

This book is primarily concerned with the practice of care by individuals in their professional roles and in the organizations of which they are a part. First, a model of care in practice is set forth to articulate a concept of care that is both inclusive enough to contain the broad range of individual and social behavior, and specific enough to distinguish care as a useful term. A review of the empirical research will explain the effect of caring and being cared for on the development of caring behaviors and attitudes in young people, as well as on other social and health outcomes. The final section will consider how we, as individuals and as a society, can be more caring toward youths and support more caring on their part.

This book focuses on organized care to middle- and high-school age youths. The concentration on youth—here defined as young people ages 12 through 18— is not meant to deny the crucial importance of caregiving and prosocial experiences in infancy and early childhood. Clearly, preadolescents and adolescents are profoundly affected by their experiences in the first decade of life. However, the dramatic development of capacities and capabilities that characterizes the first few years of life appears to require very different inputs and supports than does the gradual, but equally profound, transition from childhood to adulthood. Far less research and practical work has been done with young people, in comparison to work on early childhood, to understand their needs for caring. And yet there are likely far more untapped opportunities for adults in many walks of life to care for youths and teach them to care for themselves and others.

Much more is known about caring and its effects in infancy and early childhood than in school-age children. The role of caring in the social and emotional development of older children and adolescents has not been captured as successfully. Moreover, measures of social progress—caring for children on a societal level—focus primarily on the first few years of life. A corresponding set of indicators that focus on caring for school-age children and adolescents has yet to be developed. A set of "markers of a caring society" might include the number of adult supports available per child; the investment in education, mental health, and recreation; and the kinds of meaningful public roles available to youth.[5]

In part because their needs for care are not as obvious as those of very young children, youths often do not seem to need to be taken care of. But youths are seekers of caring. As their cognitive faculties mature, they become more able to understand and participate in the complexities of truly mutual relationships. The physical changes of adolescence create emotional volatility and intensity that can be tempered by a safe, supportive anchor. Their increasing capacities naturally seek an outlet in forays to discover new capabilities, experiment with different roles, and begin mature relationships. This period of life is also one in which an individual begins to contemplate his identity in adult society, and thus begins to develop relationships and roles outside of the family. Youths need caring adults to engage them in relationships that challenge their capacities for mutuality and respect, that provide support and stability during this process, and that model responsible, caring behavior. As research on gangs and other antisocial behavior has demonstrated, young people's needs for these relationships are so strong that they will seek them out wherever they are available.[6] If responsible adults in their lives don't provide care, youths will find it elsewhere.

The chapters that follow attempt to articulate an understanding of caring and its role in the lives of young people. Chapter 2 sets forth a definition of caring in practice. Care is presented as an active practice, the components of which interact to create an ongoing, interactive, habit of mind and action. The practice of care can be seen as a habit of action as well as the expression of an ethic. As with other practices, caring is a socially constructed practice that is determined by the cultural context in which it occurs and is influenced by cultural norms and values. This chapter will highlight some of the many assumptions that underlie mainstream American practices of care, as well as discuss some of the culturally based differences in the practice of care.

Chapter 3 will consider some of the thorny questions about care in practice. Care is an ideal; but in practice is it usually a messy, iterative process in which both the carer and the cared-for play a role. The mutuality inherent in care distinguishes it from service provision and ensures that no two care relationships are alike. Discussing the role of both parties in care relationships helps to explain how care begets caring. Trust is foundational to the capacity to care, and is itself the product of being competently cared for. Focusing on the care relationship also surfaces the tensions between caring and not caring, and the issue of boundaries to caring. How does one manage the demands of caring for large numbers of people or for very needy individuals? What are reasonable expectations for one's caregiving? What are the characteristics of responsible, competent care? How do professional caregivers avoid burnout? The ways in which caregivers address these questions can be useful indicators to both parents and young people seeking to distinguish truly caring organizations from incompetent or irresponsible caregivers.

Chapter 4 develops a framework by which to consider the development of caring in individuals. The foundations of the capacity for care are laid in early childhood, and trust is arguably the central element. Although the family is the crucial site for learning to care, young people's experiences and relationships outside the home are also important, and many can be transforming. This chapter will review the research on the impact of youth community service in developing skills and habits of care. Much of this research demonstrates that service experiences are most meaningful when they are reinforced in other social and civic contexts of a young person's life.

Chapter 5 asks the question, "What does caring really accomplish?" The aim of this chapter is to begin to develop an understanding of how caring can have an impact and to consider how such an impact can reasonably be demonstrated. This chapter will focus especially on the role of caring in the classroom and describe the processes by which some teachers have created caring environments. This section includes a review of the empirical research on the effects of being cared for on youths' health and social outcomes, on the development of caring attitudes, behaviors, and competence, and on care as a facilitating influence in learning and emotional development. In all cases in which caring is the object of study, questions arise as to how caring is measured. How does one know what caring is? Is caring best evaluated by intent or by outcome? It can be argued that care is best evaluated as a process in which the most important effects are feelings of social connectedness and an orientation toward engagement with others. These outcomes are difficult to quantify, but the model of care set forth in previous chapters might serve as a guideline for evaluation.

Chapter 6 moves from care at the individual level to caring schools and other organizations. Caring organizations are highly intentional places, devoting enormous attention to consistency between the messages they preach to young people and the messages encoded in their actions. They have institutionalized and applied caring values throughout their organization. How do caring schools and other institutions organize themselves, structure their programs, and train their staff to express and facilitate caring? What impact does a caring organization have on individual providers of care? How can organizations care for their caregiving members?

It can be argued that caring at the individual level is the essential component of social capital. In this sense, caring people aggregate into a caring society. But a caring culture implies something more: it involves social systems and interpersonal contexts that are larger than the individual and that persist over many lifespans. Individuals can imagine a "moral cosmos" of caring to include caring for social institutions and "willed commitments"—individuals or groups that are not naturally parts of one's social world. Developing a culture of caring, which is the focus of chapter 7, requires not only individual commitment, but also a reevaluation of social institutions. It is here that caring connects to social justice: the same ethic that guides face-to-face interactions becomes a template for social norms.

The final chapter is an attempt to bring what has been said about care to an examination of our society as a whole. It is hoped that the description of care at the professional and organizational level will provide some tools for considering care at the societal level. How can we work to instill values of care in both our norms of social interaction and in the very fabric of our society? What norms must be challenged in order to create a more caring society? Where is the potential for caring?

As the number of question marks in the previous pages should indicate, this book asks far more questions than it answers. It is written in the spirit of an intellectual journey, not as a guidebook of actions or remedies. There is far too much that is not known about caring and its effects for this essay to be a polemic or a manual. Rather, the reader is invited to share in the journey and "think out loud" about these and many other questions regarding caring. Wherever research is cited or others' ideas are discussed, what is not known will be pointed out along with what is. Perhaps this initial effort to understand caring and its effects will launch others in this inquiry, if only to repudiate the arguments presented here.

CHAPTER 2

The Practice of Care

It is the fourth day of the National Indian Youth Leadership Project's annual summer camp, and sixty or seventy young people are gathered in a clearing to begin an all-day hike. The youths and the adults with them have been assigned to clans for the week; each clan will hike in a different direction and report on what they see. It is a beautiful July morning, and Camp Asaayi, seven miles down a dirt road in the Navajo Nation in New Mexico, is a remote and picturesque spot. But McClellan Hall, NIYLP's executive director and the leader of Clan 4, implores the youths not to be tourists on this hike. "This is your land," he says. "Your ancestors probably lived in a place a lot like this. You belong to this land as much as any mountain lion or chipmunk, any tree or flower you see."

The National Indian Youth Leadership Project, based in Gallup, New Mexico, was founded to offer young Native Americans opportunities to develop interests that are positive outlets for their energies and avenues to reconnect with their cultural traditions. Most of the Project's work centers on the Zuni and Navajo youths in Gallup and surrounding reservations, where NIYLP works intensively with middle school students in leadership and outdoor adventure programs. The programs are part of a highly successful substance abuse prevention program in which drugs and alcohol are never discussed. "Most prevention programs say 'Don't do this, don't do that,'" explains Mac Hall. "But we learned from the elders that the traditional way of teaching is not to confront things head on; you have to work indirectly with negative things. So our approach is, 'What else could you do?'"

NIYLP has focused on wilderness adventure programs and service projects as a means to develop leadership, self-esteem, and values of cooperation and interdependence. The Project runs afterschool climbing and outdoors clubs, takes middle school children on camping trips and other outdoor adventures, and sponsors accredited search-and-rescue teams for high school-age youths. In the summertime, the middle schoolers from New Mexico are joined by Native American youths from other parts of the country in an eight-day camp designed to promote cultural exchange among tribes and reinforce the lessons of the school year. Twelve-, thirteen-, and fourteen-year-olds come as campers; older adolescents come as "service staff" and are meant to be role models to the younger children.

Although most of the youths at the summer camp are from rural areas, few have had much experience in the wilderness. Mac is trying to take them out of themselves, hoping that they will relax and begin to observe the world around them, a world he believes they are traditionally, viscerally connected to. "You know what tourists do: they make lots of noise, ignore others around them, break stuff or destroy things thoughtlessly. Don't be a tourist: walk this land like you own it."

The clans are lined up facing each other in each of the four directions of the compass. Mac describes the Native American mythology of the four directions, offering lots of caveats about the different beliefs of different tribes. Then Alfred, a local volunteer, leads a Navajo prayer for the morning. The young people are all silent and respectful; they take their hats off, and face east; but it's not clear what, if anything, they are getting from this. Most are not Navajo: the camp recruits Native American youths from as far away as Minnesota and Florida; of those that are Navajo, many do not speak the Navajo language. "It might be that what's most important about these experiences is that they're a chance for young people to see that Native American culture is respected, and to learn that they can participate, in their own way, in their cultural tradition," explained Cheryl Lovett-Green, a founding board member of NIYLP. "This isn't meant to be a cultural reimmersion program; but it is meant to be an opportunity to learn to respect what you are."

Mac Hall described what many of the camp's participants are up against:

Our kids are being influenced by the media and the dominant culture without, in many cases, much connection to their traditional values . . . you have to remember that this might be the first generation raised at home: their parents and grandparents were probably shipped off to boarding schools in different times, so many do not have a strong home life or strong community . . . and racism is so ingrained that the kids that are more connected to their culture are made fun of by the less traditional ones.

At Camp Asaayi, participants are asked not to bring clothing that glorifies drugs or alcohol, and radios, televisions, even soda cans are nowhere to be found. All NIYLP staff must pledge to abstain from drugs, including alcohol and tobacco, for the duration of their employment. The day begins with calisthenics and a run, and activities are geared toward nature and the outdoors. It is all part of a strategy to free young people from influences that, in NIYLP's view, have limited their potential and robbed their imagination. "The whole essence of the camp is creating a community for a week to give you a feel for what it could be like if everybody worked together and practiced some of those traditional values," explained Mac Hall. "A lot of it is not a direct message; it is an indirect thing, and you take from it what you are ready to absorb."

On the trail, the fifteen youths in Clan 4 don't appear to have been much influenced by Mac's imprecations not to be a tourist. They throw rocks in the water, shout back and forth, and run ahead despite requests to stay together. When Mac stops to show them mullein, a native plant traditionally used for toilet paper, they shout and joke in embarrassment. But as the walk progresses, they grow quieter and more observant; when Mac points out a brown trout spawning under a rock, they watch silently and intently for many minutes.

The hike is long, and many of the young people pick out walking sticks as they go. As the day progresses, a number of the group, including most of the boys and young men, have wrapped bouquets of wildflowers around the top of their sticks. "I don't think there's many places you'd see a 16- or 17-year-old boy pick flowers," points out Kevin Metallic, a Mi'g Maq Indian from Canada who is working for NIYLP this summer. "In their communities, there are pretty strong negative images of how you're supposed to act."

"For many of these young people, this might be the first place where they can be positive and people will respect that," said Cheryl Lovett-Green.

Tina, a heavyset young woman from Minnesota, isn't enjoying the hike or, she declares, the whole camp experience. When asked why, she gives sidelong, angry glances at Mac Hall. She doesn't like the routine, the lack of freedom, the joint activities. Tina looks older than her 13 years and refuses to engage in any of the play or banter of the other youths on the hike. She stumbles along, hunched over; at times, she asks if she can stop and wait till the group circles back in the afternoon. She complains of an impending migraine. When, after three hours of hiking, she trips on a root, she crumbles to the ground and bursts into tears.

Mac comes over to help her, kindly but not overly solicitous. In fact, he seems somewhat detached, responsive to Tina's injury but barely acknowledging her distress. She isn't seriously hurt, but she's very upset. Mac suggests she put her ankle in the stream, and moves a log into place for her to sit on, but he doesn't bring her to the stream himself. When she's rested awhile, he helps her get ready to go, but makes it clear she'll have to walk herself. For the rest of the hike, Mac walks with Tina, directing the group to stop at intervals so that Tina can soak her ankle in the stream again. Tina is grim, resolute, but not crying anymore.

Later, Mac explained his behavior:

> Tina did really well this afternoon. I was expecting something like this . . . you should have seen her medical form . . . The other day I overheard her boasting that when she gets migraines she pretty much gets to decide what she wants to do, so I caught on to that stuff right away. Earlier today I went over to her and I put my arm on her shoulder and said, 'You know, everybody wants you to be here. We are trying to make you feel welcome, and I saw you playing lacrosse out there, you are not fooling anybody, we know you can run. You need to get into it and let yourself have fun.' . . So I didn't let her get away with too much, but at the same time I don't want to be insensitive . . . She was wanting sympathy, I think—but today I felt like she earned some respect because she walked out by herself after she got hurt . . . and she was pretty tough.

Pointing out plants and animal tracks, Mac is still the center of the hike; he directs many of his observations first to Tina, and she appears more and more engaged. By the end of the hike, she has joined some of the others who are teaching each other words in their different tribal languages. By dinnertime, when Clan 4 is in charge of serving the rest of the camp, Tina is spooning out coleslaw and laughing with her clanmates.

After dinner, the camp assembles to hear reports from each clan. One group has brought back a dozen plants with traditional uses; many of the young people in this group had learned about the plants from a grandparent or local elder. Each group has been given a set of questions to reflect on their experience. Although some have taken the assignment quite seriously, others do not appear to have given the questions much thought. Still, the meeting goes on for quite a while, with many individuals standing to give testimonial to personal epiphanies or private observations. At last, Mac stands and recounts to the group the traditional significance of finding a bird feather. He then describes Tina's ordeal, declares how proud he is of her, and presents her with a hawk feather he has found. The next day, her ankle wrapped, Tina is beaming. She cannot go on the hike today, to the prehistoric ruins of Canyon De Chey, but she has asked to be taken as far as possible in the car. Now, Tina says, camp is fun. "I was just getting sucked into a negative attitude," she explains.

"We used to joke about it," said Cheryl Lovett-Green, "That anyone who was trouble at the beginning would be one that we'd want back as service staff the next summer." Some campers return as service staff and develop ongoing affiliations with NIYLP. The camp relies heavily on the service of teens, who are meant to be role models "of real teenagers, not the picture-perfect Native culture," explained Cheryl. The role of older teens is integral to the NIYLP model of service. "The idea of the multilevel, intergenerational role modeling that is going on is to show kids how each one sort of owes something to the next one down," said Mac Hall. "We are giving kids the idea that in order for the community to work, there is an expectation that everybody has to do their part." For the older teens, many of whom have been at NIYLP summer camps for several years, the service position is training in traditional values of leadership in which service and responsibility are paramount.

The NIYLP camp is only a week long, and Mac freely admits that its effects have more to do with the young person than with the program. "You light the spark, and if they are ready they will really take off, and if they are not, they will take a little bit of it back," he said. But even in the more sustained programs during the school year, NIYLP's philosophy appears not to be driven by standardized results. The drug and alcohol prevention programs, the leadership camps, and the service training are organized not to teach specific skills or change particular behaviors but to affect development in a most individualized and subtle fashion. "You are sort of planting a seed," explained Mac Hall. "You have to understand that they are going to get this lesson when they are developmentally ready, and that might be in a week or a few years."

*   *   *

Caring—the "stuff" behind transforming experiences and relationships—is at once a mundane practice and the embodiment of an abstract ideal. Fundamentally, care is a practice: it happens in real time, and it is tangible. Although the practice of care can be spoken of in general terms, each instance of care is caring precisely because it is a specific response to a particular situation. For care is, by definition, not about prescribed behaviors or attitudes, but about responding to others in the context of their individual needs and desires.

The experience of practicing care in particular contexts develops a habit of caring. A habit of care is a habit of action, but also a habit of mind. It can be thought of as an ethic of care, a philosophy of accepting and rejoicing in one's responsibilities to others and to groups and organizations. In this respect, caring is more than a practice: it is the expression of a social ideal.

This chapter will attempt to describe the actions, capacities, and attitudes that comprise the practice of care. Care can be described as the interplay of attentiveness, responsiveness, and competence. This model of care distinguishes between caring *for*, which is essentially active, and caring *about*, which is not necessarily so, focusing solely on the former. However, it makes no distinction between "disinterested" care and care motivated in part by self-interest. Practically, it is usually impossible to discern the motives of another, and of little or no value. If one conceptualizes care as a practice that occurs in the interactions of people, rather than inside the head of the carer, the focus naturally shifts from motivation to questions of appropriate action and responsiveness. It is sufficient to say that care happens, without considering its value based on the intent of the caregiver.

A central assumption is that care, expressed as a habit of action, is also a habit of mind. What does it mean to hold an ethic of care, and how might that ethic be expressed in action and attitude? What is the connection between particular instances of caregiving and a philosophy of care?

Finally, inasmuch as care is a practice, it is shaped by and responsive to the needs and expectations of a culture, a term here used broadly to include both nation-states and ethnic and socioeconomic subcultures in the United States. There are universals to caring behavior, expressed somewhat differently by different cultures. Caring for children and youth, in particular, is a process of shaping them and preparing them to perform in society. Every culture has a unique vision of the ideal capacities and attributes of an adult, as well as a distinct set of challenges for development. The way care is practiced in any culture is both an expression of the values of the culture and an attempt to optimize development for a young person in that society. Cultures differ in the extent to which they emphasize the individual over the community, abstract versus concrete skills, and nuclear versus extended families, among other things. Such different perspectives lead to divergent expectations about both the provision of care and the behaviors and capacities of young people.

A MODEL OF CARE: ATTENTIVENESS, RESPONSIVENESS, AND COMPETENCE

It is commonplace to think of care as synonymous with comfort, concern, or kindness. But this definition must be extended in order to be meaningful. In practice, care is more discriminating, a product of skill and judgment as well as emotion. Care can be described as an endlessly cycling process comprised of three interrelated components: attentiveness, responsiveness, and competence, all of which are necessary and none alone sufficient for caring.[1]

The quality of *attentiveness* highlights the importance of "otherness" in care.

It involves concern for others, awareness of other people's needs, desires, and suffering, and the ability to consider others' points of view. It is what the philosopher and educator Nel Noddings describes when, quoting Kierkegaard, she speaks of "apprehending the reality of the other."[2] It is both a state of being receptive to others and of mental clarity, or awareness, that allows one to see not only what one expects to see, but what is truly there. Attentiveness is not merely a passive state of readiness for whatever might come along; it is the active seeking of an understanding of the other.

In attending to the other, we focus on the singularity of the other rather than on a comparison between him and us. His otherness, rather than repelling us or keeping us apart, is accepted as a necessity of his being not us. It is extremely hard to focus on the other with respect and to think about his qualities in terms other than his differences from ourselves. That is perhaps why we are so much more capable of caring for our own group than we are for someone outside the group.

Attentiveness is essential in the practice of care because it is the process by which one gathers the information necessary to make a "diagnosis" of the needs of another. Caring behaviors without attentiveness are mechanical functions, often inappropriate to the needs of the other. A lack of attentiveness is a lack of respect, as though the other were not worthy of being considered as a unique individual. Caring requires an attention to each person as a unique individual, and, therefore, the investment in time and effort required to come to know a young person. It was Mac Hall's attentiveness to Tina's attitudes, medical history, and self-concept than enabled him to respond effectively to her injury, in a way that both supported and challenged her. Without having observed Tina in social situations and watched her response to other challenges, Mac might not have been able to spur her on to participate in and enjoy the camp.

One cannot be focused on oneself and be truly attentive. For example, a parent who cares only that her own aspirations be realized in her child, despite the interests and wishes of the child, is caring for the needs of her own ego rather than those of the child. Her failure to attend to the child's wishes, instead of her own, indicates her failure of caregiving.

Responsiveness, the motivation to do the caring behavior itself, is another essential component of care. Responsiveness speaks to motivation without proscribing a value to one's intent. Responsiveness reflects the necessity of caring, regardless of whether that necessity springs from principle, duty, or affect. As such, it might be a primarily emotional or primarily rational process, depending on the situation and the individuals involved. It is responsiveness that impels us to act: to call out to a stranger who has unknowingly dropped his wallet; to reach out to a woman who has fallen and appears to need help; to embrace a child who begins to cry. With attentiveness, we go beyond ourselves to the other in our state of mind; with responsiveness, we extend ourselves to act to help another.

Like attentiveness and competence, responsiveness is both a feature of particular situations of care and transferable across contexts. Responsiveness is a habit of action just as attentiveness is a habit of mind; but this fact does not imply that one is responsive all the time. One can be attitudinally programmed to respond and can be more or less in the habit of responding. While no one is caring all of the time, some people are more "in practice" than others.

Having attended and responded to the needs and desires of the other, competent care meets a need—whether or not it is recognized and identified by the one cared for. *Competence* is relevant both to the assessment of the necessary action and to the doing of the action itself. Unlike most philosophical takes on virtue, competence is neither a state of mind nor a way of thought. It is a skill that clearly has both cognitive and affective qualities. It is knowing what to say and how to say it, or what to do and how to do it. It is knowing, and being able, to refrain from action when one's strongest affective impulses are to action. It is knowing, as well, the *value* of the care one can offer to its recipient. This aspect of care is perhaps easiest to imagine in terms of an Aristotelian virtue: competence in care can be taught and cultivated, and it is certainly a product of experience.

Caring is not usually considered a skill, but many of the processes involved in caring rely on capabilities that come naturally to some and require effort by others. We tend to think of such attributes as empathy and expressiveness as personal qualities, when in fact they are skills of successful social interaction. Competence also involves knowledge and rational thought. If attentiveness suggests awareness and appreciation for the other as an other, competence suggests knowledge of the other and the context of his needs, capabilities, and situation that are derived from experience and thought. Mac, for example, chose to give Tina some comfort when she hurt her ankle, but at the same time nurtured and supported her ability to complete the hike. Thus, he was able to care enough—and well enough—to help her get the immediate care she needed and get the most out of the entire experience.

Cheryl Lovett-Green described how many of the service staff at the NIYLP summer camp "need ongoing guidance and support in dealing with all kinds of issues. For example, some of the younger kids will develop crushes on the service staff and they [the service staff] need help learning how to establish boundaries that allow them to maintain the relationship without having it go too far."

Competence is an essential component of caring, but it is more a state of being than a fixed quality. Caregivers are competent to varying degrees; they will need certain skills for some groups and different skills for others. As important as natural abilities is an ongoing commitment to develop skills that might make one more empathic and effective: to learn Spanish, for example, if one has chosen to work with Latino youths; or to find support systems for abused children if one suspects that a youth has been abused. This commitment to developing competence requires, as well, a commitment to assessing one's capacities and shortcomings as a caregiver. Part of competence, then, is learning the situations in which one might be most capable of caring and being willing to work to develop new capabilities.

The final and, in a sense, most important quality of the caring process is the interactive nature of its three components. As attentiveness prepares a way for responsiveness, and responsiveness demands competence, they each circle back to one another. There is no definable cycle of a caring process: by definition, the consideration of the effect of one's action must be connected to the doing of the action itself. Caring requires that the carer consider the impact of his actions on the one cared for. Such consideration is integral to and consistent with the ethic of respecting the integrity and uniqueness of the other as an individual with a value equal to one's own.

A picture of interactive, iterative caring suggests an ongoing process rather than a single action at a point in time. And in fact, most, though not all, of our caring actions are performed in the context of an ongoing relationship in which one responds, and attends, and then considers the necessity of responding again. Continuity—the ongoing relationship between the carer and cared for—and its sister, constancy—the commitment that the care will be available when needed—are important defining characteristics of care. Together, they are what bind individual acts of kindness into caring relationships that support growth and development. One cannot feel cared for if the care is haphazard and unreliable, or if one does not know that the carer will attend to one's response to his care and offer a response in return. It is this knowledge that allows infants to develop trust in the external world and, eventually, in themselves; likewise, it is this knowledge that allows us to place our trust in specific people with whom we develop relationships. The connections between trust and constancy suggest that there are cumulative effects to caring that cannot be captured in a description of caring as a discrete transaction.

Infusing the practice of caring—attentiveness, responsiveness, and competence—is will, consciousness, and deliberateness of action and commitment to expending energy and effort. The practice of care does not happen effortlessly. It might not be the case that all forms of care require sacrifice—certainly many produce such joy that the sacrifice is not apparent—but all require effort, and thus all require will. Whereas some components of the caring process draw on affective processes, and others more on cognitive abilities, all require that one direct one's will toward the effort of paying attention, of thinking, of acting, and of paying attention again.

CARE: A HABIT OF ACTION

Although care cannot be evaluated on the basis of motivations, it is important to explore how one becomes inclined to care. Much of the writing on care has referred to the carer's affective response—feelings and emotional reaction—as the motivator for caring behavior. Although there is clearly an affective component to care, it is important that care not be defined solely in terms of emotion. There must be some principle or ideal as motivator as well. One does not always care to satisfy a feeling aroused in oneself: to define care in that way is to equate it with any number of practices that satisfy personal urges or inclinations. Because care is a practice embedded in and arising from a social context, it does not necessarily imply a universalistic moral order. Yet as caring behaviors become habit, they suggest an underlying orientation, a point of view, that one might consider a guiding ethic.

The phrase "an ethic of care" has great currency among feminist scholars, communitarians, and other virtue-based philosophers. It arises from Carol Gilligan's seminal work on the moral reasoning of women, undertaken in response to her mentor Lawrence Kohlberg's famous six-stage model of moral development.[3] Kohlberg's model was derived from experimental situations in which subjects (exclusively boys and men) were asked to explain their decision making in a variety of hypothetical situations. Kohlberg's model describes the highest level of moral reasoning as occurring on an abstract plane in which justice and equality of rights are the primary considerations. In contrast to Kohlberg's justice orientation, Gilligan found that her female subjects spoke of their real-life moral dilemmas in terms of the specifics of the relationships involved and the importance of caring for themselves and others. Gilligan termed this feminine moral reasoning "an ethic of care," and contrasted its foundation of relatedness and responsiveness to others with an "ethic of justice" based on autonomy and abstract reasoning. In the years since her research was first published in 1977, Gilligan's ideas have spawned research in a wide range of fields, including psychology, philosophy, law, and social theory. Some have challenged her findings, and others have questioned the extent to which differences in moral orientation can, and should, be related to gender. Nonetheless, the impact of her thesis has been widespread and profound.

Viewing care as a practice offers a slightly different perspective. An ethic of care can be considered the habit, or disposition, toward attentiveness and responsiveness, instead of a moral argument. In the context of social action, an ethic of care can be considered a disposition to approach self, group, and society from a point of view that values interdependence, respects the uniqueness of others, and considers individuals from a holistic perspective. An ethic of care is as much a way of approaching interactions and viewing relationships as it is a guideline for moral behavior.

One philosopher has described caring as "the disposition to respond to others and the world as worthy of engagement."[4] There is, in an ethic of care, an orientation toward active involvement in the maintenance and well-being of the social organizations of which one is a part—not only to one's intimate others, but to the larger social systems that comprise one's world. In its orientation toward attentiveness and responsiveness, as well as its value of interdependence, an ethic of care compels one toward participation in large-scale systems that value the individual, respect otherness, and celebrate the connectedness that arises from shared enterprises. In this way, care relates directly to citizenship in its most idealized and fully realized form. This is how a program like the National Indian Youth Leadership Project can address the development of leadership skills for a community through the experience of caring for clan members and fellow youths.

THE CULTURAL CONTENT OF CARE

The practice of care is situated in, and determined by, the cultural context in which it occurs. The way that care is practiced in a culture is both an expression of what that culture values and the means by which these values are sustained across generations. Care for children, in particular, serves both to protect them and to socialize them to take on adult roles in their society. Effective care can be thought of as a process of optimizing the development of the individual with respect to the society of which he or she is a part. The optimal outcome of development—the attributes and abilities of the adult—will vary according to the roles, values, and expectations of the time and culture.

The practice of care is influenced by cultural norms and values, some of which are deeply rooted, abstract ideas so taken for granted as to be rarely articulated. For example, the way we behave toward our children is based in some part on how we understand cause and effect in development. Common theories of how social practices affect outcomes—the conviction that things happen for a discernible reason, and that anything can be changed with effective, substantial effort—are deeply rooted in Western intellectual and religious traditions. Mainstream American consciousness is so grounded in the abstract, logical reasoning of the Age of Enlightenment that it is often difficult to remember that such thinking does not dominate all cultures. In fact, a mystical, divinely inspired worldview was the prevailing mode of thought for most of history. It is only since the discoveries of Galileo and Newton that we have expected to understand the physical world and human interactions as predictable, explainable phenomena. We have come to see rational order as the organizing force of not only science and markets, but interpersonal relations as well.

Western culture has glorified rational thought to such an extent that care has been subsumed into formal, abstract norms of moral reasoning and of moral development. As the philosopher Alisdair MacIntyre has noted, the study and discussion of ethics in Western philosophy has been dominated by the views of the eighteenth-century philosopher Immanuel Kant since the publication of *Critique of Pure Reason* in 1781.[5] Kant developed a moral order of universal, abstract, formal principles, analogous to the laws of physics. He argued that right and wrong could be assessed solely by examining the motives of an actor, without regard to the particulars of the situation. This is a very abstract notion of care, indeed; and far from a practical view of caring as grounded in the specifics of a relationship and an individual's needs. However, Kant's perspective has influenced norms of moral reasoning and of moral development, contributing to a feeling that caring is soft and intellectually imprecise. Moreover, the justifications for actions, rather than the actions themselves, continue to dominate discussions of what constitutes proper human interaction. As philosophers such as MacIntyre and Joan Tronto have pointed out, the "moral point of view" privileges morality as an autonomous sphere of human life, untouched by social and political connections, and beyond emotions and feelings.[6]

The way in which care is practiced in different cultures also relates to beliefs about morality, human nature, and the assumed and proper motivations for good deeds. When people believed the world to be divinely inspired, man was viewed as divine as well. As Enlightenment thinkers and early scientists demonstrated that man is an animal, so stripped of his divine associations, it was assumed he must act as an animal as well. In place of a divinely inspired humanity, some philosophers promoted an image of an egoistic, brutal mankind whose natural impulses are to power and the satisfaction of one's own desires. The "natural state of man" described in Thomas Hobbes *Leviathan*, published in 1651, is an important artifact of Western cultural consciousness. Hobbes describes a humankind as being driven by two fundamental motives: the desire to dominate and the desire to avoid death. "Men from their very birth, and naturally, scramble for everything they covet, and would have all the world, if they could, to fear and obey them."[7] Perhaps Freud has been most influential in shaping our view of essential human instincts as driven toward "primary mutual hostility."[8]

Modern psychobiologists, sociobiologists, and other human scientists have sought to understand the occurrence of care in society by reference to the biological concept of altruism. In its technical, biological sense, altruism refers to behavior that is detrimental to an individual organism but can be shown to have positive effects on the continuation of a genotype. In the animal world, such behavior is generally thought to be instinctual rather than motivated by reason or volition. The human sciences, however, have appropriated the behavioral definition of altruism and included the notion of volition and motivation to distinguish "genuine altruism" from altruism motivated by genetic selection. As Trivers has observed, models "that attempt to explain altruistic behavior in terms of natural selection are models designed to take the altruism out of altruism."[9] Not surprisingly, through this perspective, the field of evolutionary psychology has concluded that there is no such thing as "genuine" altruism, and that those who believe they are acting for motives other than self-interest are kidding themselves.

Thus, in mainstream American culture, care is viewed in a context that stresses rationality, individual choice, formal notions of right and wrong, and a primarily self-serving human nature. These beliefs and attitudes inform our understanding of what caring is and how it is demonstrated. They also shape culturally specific practices of care and influence what we teach about caring.

Perhaps the best example of the cultural relativity of care is the degree to which individuality is developed and valued. Although all care is individually focused, societies do not all view the maximization of individuality as an equally desirable outcome of care. The universalist, moral point of view assumes that the meaningful unit of action in moral decisions is the individual. Each individual is presumed to have an autonomous set of interests and to be able to consider his interests independent of others' concerns. While sentiments or concerns for others might, for some philosophers, enter into moral judgments, the moral point of view presumes that each individual's situation can be considered independently. It is important to note that this privilege is a cultural construct, not a fact of human nature. Cross-cultural research into the nature of self has shown that people's notions of self-interest and of the boundaries that separate self from others vary greatly among cultures.[10] The Western notion of the self as an independent, autonomous entity has become such a presumption in our thinking that we are often unaware of how culturally specific it is.

Care is also very much connected to a culture's values and myths. For example, our expectations of care and caregiving are based, in part, on how we conceptualize the life cycle. In modern society, we segment childhood and old age as distinct periods of life separated from the current of everyday public and, to some extent, private life; and we have created specialized institutions and caregivers to serve these populations. However, this situation is relatively modern. The notion of childhood as a unique phase of life did not exist before the sixteenth century, and it was only in the Victorian era that children were seen as morally and emotionally vulnerable and in need of protection from the influences of the external world.[11] Similarly, the concept of adolescence as a separate developmental experience, with its own emotional terrain, culture, and patterns of experience, is an even more modern concept, developing—depending on the point of view of different researchers—in the early twentieth century or as late as the 1950s.[12] Modern segmentation of the life cycle has led to some degree of ambivalence about the proper public role in care for children. It has also led to a sense of disconnection between the work and experience of adulthood and that of childhood.

Similarly, the practice of care is determined in great part by cultural expectations for social roles of family members and outsiders. These expectations are constantly evolving: American society has seen some change over the past decades with respect to the role of fathers in care for children. At the same time, increased opportunities for women to work outside the home and expanding geographic mobility have changed expectations of child care from other members of the nuclear and extended family. Smaller families and a greater focus on experiences and opportunities outside the home have also changed the dynamics of sibling caretaking. Modern, Western practices of care for young children (and the psychosocial research that examines it) rarely consider caretaking of children by siblings. Yet child and sibling caretaking is either the norm or a significant form of caretaking in most societies throughout the world.[13]

The degree to which children are seen as a collective responsibility of a society versus the private property of their parents is also a cultural phenomenon. The role of children in the economic support and security of their families in early rural America has left its legacy in a legal system in which children historically have had few rights with respect to their parents. As discussed above, the nuclear family has evolved to a position not only of primacy, but of isolation in child-rearing. In contrast to cultures in which child care is more diffuse, American culture places an extraordinary weight on the nuclear family as the provider of care.

However, the United States is not a monolithic society, but rather an amalgamation of racial, ethnic, and socioeconomic groupings with varying degrees of culturally derived distinctions in values, family dynamics, rituals, and social groupings, among other things. Although there are clearly universal elements to care, the social structures by which young people are cared for and the actions and attitudes by which such care is expressed do vary across cultural subgroups.

Some culturally based differences in structures and styles of care provision have been explored in psychological and sociological research. The cultural roots and socioeconomic determinants of African American caregiving and family structure have begun to receive serious study.[14] Patricia Collins has described the African American tradition of "othermothering," which she claims arises from West African polygamous extended families.[15] This custom of kin and non-kin women sharing the upbringing of children, Collins suggests, offers a network model of care bonds that can be a healthy alternative to the mainstream nuclear family structure. Othermothering contrasts with the predominant focus on the mother-child dyad in most mainstream psychological research. Similarly, an appreciation of caring practices as adaptive to particular social environments has led some scholars to propose that white middle-class norms for parenting styles are not adaptive for dangerous inner-city environments. Parents in these contexts might most effectively protect their children from both physical dangers in inner-city environments and emotional challenges relating to racism and discrimination through a highly authoritarian, overprotective caregiving style that emphasizes discipline over affection.[16]

There has been very little empirical examination of whether perceptions of caring actions differ across racial or ethnic groups. One study of middle school students' perceptions of caring teachers found that African-American students were more likely to offer interpersonal attributes as markers of caring, while white students more frequently described instrumental attributes, such as helping with homework and offering advice.[17] However, a similar study of middle school children found no racial differences.[18] Spontaneous and unforced sharing has been noted as more common among inner-city African-American children than in their white middle-class counterparts. The Kansas City Block Brothers, who are all African American, frequently mentioned sharing money with their charges as a part of their care for them.

The experiences of different racial and ethnic subgroups and of cultures in other countries highlight the importance of definitional flexibility in caring. The universal components of care—attentiveness, responsiveness, and competence—are not likely to appear the same in different cultures. Moreover, the activities of care will serve culturally specific ends. We should expect care to be adaptive to particular cultures and to reflect the values and desired developmental outcomes of the culture. A model of care in practice, however, should allow us to identify and assess very different expressions of caring behaviors.

CHAPTER 3

MUTUALITY, TRUST, AND BOUNDARIES

The high school students who frequent The Warming House, a drop-in center in an upper middle-class suburb of Chicago, call it "a second home," "a refuge," "a place to recharge," but for some, at some times, it is more than that. Max started coming with a friend in the middle of his sophomore year, "just for fun, because it was a new place to hang out," but soon thereafter found himself needing support:

> It was in the time before my dad moved out: my parents were separating, and my dad really took it out on me. He was really abusive . . . I come from a very conservative family, where the father is king, so my mom really couldn't do very much . . . I needed someone to talk to, just to understand so I wouldn't be angry all the time . . . I would come here, talk to Wendy, build myself up . . . and get ready to go home for Round 2.

The Warming House takes its name from its former function as the head-quarters for an outdoor skating rink, now replaced by a soccer field. When the center moved to the building, the staff decided the original name was appropriate for the kind of environment they hoped to create. The Warming House is a drop-in center open to all ninth through twelfth graders in the township, but catering particularly to young people vulnerable to stress and distress. Although the center has been in operation for twenty-five years, it isn't highly visible in this well-to-do suburb. "Here on the North Shore, there's a real ambivalence about centers like these," explained a youth worker at the local junior high school. "There's some idea that 'good' kids don't need help from anyone outside their family—but of course everyone does, at some point." And the material success that supports the well-kept lawns and chic storefronts takes its toll on the young people struggling to find an identity in their community. Most of the young people at The Warming House attend New Trier High School, known as one of the best and most competitive public high schools in the country. "Oh gosh, when I am in school I feel like so much is on my shoulders. I have this due and that due," one young man said. "Period after period I feel like everything is falling on top of me and I can't handle it."

"If you just drive your car around here, you can see that there is a standard of living here," said one administrator, "and the teens know that if they want to continue to live in the life style that they're accustomed to that they'll have to do something close to what their parents did. Some are more aware of this than others, and some are so aware that they just turn away. . . . And some of the kids are terrified."

The young people who visit this drop-in center are difficult to categorize. Although all are middle class, they're of differing social and ethnic backgrounds. Their family situations differ: some come from broken or neglectful families, but others describe strong, positive relationships with their parents. Most seem outspoken and eager to please; but as a group, they appear defiant and challenging. Many present angry, troubled faces to outsiders; most of the youths smoke cigarettes and dress in grunge clothing; cursing and acting out are common. "We're not your typical suburban teenagers in Gap clothes," explains Elizabeth, a senior. "We're kind of scary." And yet these young people in particular seem to need a place where they are accepted by people who take the time to see past their defiant facades. Like most adolescents, the young people at The Warming House seem at once proud and anxious that they are not "typical." Most of all, they seem relieved to fit in at The Warming House.

"It's not like school," said Missy, a junior. "Here, people just accept you for who you are."

At first glance, it appears that nothing much is going on at The Warming House, other than teenagers being teenagers. The center is housed in a small cinderblock building. A Ping-Pong table, a pool table, and a punching bag take over most of the main room. Old couches are arranged around a television, and a pair of giant speakers vibrate with alternative rock. A separate room is rimmed with couches on which young people are sprawled, some doing their homework. Murals cover all the walls, except for one devoted to photographs, letters, and fliers. "This is meant to be a place where kids can just *be*," said Cindy Nash, executive director of the Warming House from 1994 to 1998, "but protected by safety, consistency, and adults who genuinely care about them."

The Warming House is both physically safe—adult supervision prohibits drug use, fights, and any gang behavior—and emotionally safe. Conversations with staff are kept strictly confidential, even from parents.

An atmosphere of acceptance helps all young people feel as though they belong. "Everyone just loves each other here," said one young man. "At school, we all might be in different cliques, but here, we all look out for each other."

Scheduled activities, including volunteering at the senior center and the police department, field trips, and art projects, are offered for youths who need structure and involvement. But most young people seem to come to hang out and to talk to staff who accept them and take interest in them. "All the kids that come here are looking for structured support, they are looking for role models, and they are looking for someone to really care about what they are doing with their lives and where they are going," explained Cindy Nash. "But before any healthy change is going to take place, before you can explore who they are or what they do, you have to build a relationship."

Building relationships with young people is process that unfolds at the teen's pace. "Different kids have different strategies," explained Laura Rodenkirch, a staff member in her early twenties. "Some kids do the 'dump and run:' they tell you their story, and then wait to see if you produce the appropriate reaction. Others wait and watch you interact with other kids, and then decide you're safe to talk to." Staff try to make themselves approachable by demonstrating acceptance and empathy.

Like most youth workers, the staff at The Warming House have found that it is easier to build relationships in the context of activities than in isolated "counseling" encounters. Repetitive, unthreatening activities, such as playing pool, helping with homework, or watching television together, can serve as vehicles for developing relationships. As Cindy Nash described,

> We do a lot of letting the kids be where they are, at the level they are. At first there is a lot of small talk and a lot of Ping-Pong, but then the kids get comfortable and they know that the staff will react consistently, so then maybe they will open up and talk, and we will always be there for them. But we don't fish for information.

Max described how he became comfortable enough with Wendy, a staff member at The Warming House, to begin to confide in her about his family problems:

> Every time I'd come in she'd come up and greet me and say, "Hi, how's it going?" and when I didn't look so good she'd say, "You look kind of sad

today—what's going on?" And so it wasn't so hard to start to tell her, "Well, I'm having some problems with my dad . . ." But you have to bring it up. She talked to me only when I wanted to talk.

Another young man said, "They let anyone in here, but you are not nobody when you come in." A high school junior described why he felt comfortable talking to the staff:

Well, a lot of times you don't talk to people because you feel like they might take advantage of you, or they might use your vulnerability against you, but you can trust them [the staff]; it's not like your grades matter or they have obligations to your parents or anyone.

The ease with which these young people describe their relationships with the staff at The Warming House belie the tremendous effort that caring adults put into these relationships. The cycle of caring—attention, responsiveness, and competence—is hard work. Really listening to a young person and reading a face to understand a state of mind is a habit of attention that requires continual effort. And the commitment to engage when there is trouble in a young person's eyes is a major responsibility, considering that the problem might be unpleasant or messy, the young person's understanding flawed or limited, and the likelihood of ongoing involvement high.

The staff at the Warming House manage this effort in several ways. First, although the Center is not technically a counseling center, all of the staff have counseling backgrounds and use the standards of the therapeutic relationship as boundaries for their relationships with the young people. Staff are not allowed to give teens rides, loan them money, or socialize with them outside of Warming House activities, although staff sometimes attend teens' performances or sporting events at school. These boundaries help staff manage some of the more disruptive or troubled youths, protecting the staff from complicity in any dangerous or illegal activities on the part of a young person while allowing them to maintain an unconditionally supportive relationship. "If a kid asks me for money—I don't know what he's going to do with it—I can say, 'Sorry, man, you know the rules,'" explained one staff member, gesturing to the wall painted with the Center rules.

Another important boundary is that the relationship between a young person and staff member ends when the staff member leaves or the young person graduates from high school. Although this rule is often hard on young people and staff members alike, the Center believes the termination process is an important growth experience for the teens. "Being able to manage the separation, letting go and moving on, are adult life skills," explained Cindy Nash. The

Warming House makes a special event of graduation, when seniors are no longer able to come to the Center, and holds ceremonies to mark the departure of every staff member. These events are very emotional and highly memorable. Each staff member is expected to write a letter to the teens describing his or her feelings about the place, and these letters remain on the walls for years. Staff members also say personal goodbyes to teens, and these too are opportunities to offer inspiration and guidance to young people. Tim, a junior, described his leave-taking of Adrienne, his favorite staffer:

> She called me "her knight in shining armor." No one ever said something like that to me. I know my parents love me, but they never really said special things like that to me. It made me feel so good. I was on top of the world for the rest of that night, and it still makes me feel good just thinking about it.

Drawing on their training in counseling, the staff at The Warming House also work to manage their own feelings about the teens they see. Adolescents are particularly challenging to work with because, as one youth worker said, "I believe there's an unresolved teenager in all of us." Staff regularly share among themselves frustrations with particular situations and young people with an eye to understanding how their own experiences in adolescence are affecting their interactions with the youths. Acknowledging the impact of their own experiences allows staff members to separate their own feelings from the needs of the young person at hand. Cindy Nash explains:

> We talk all the time, among the staff, about what that teen makes you think, or what this teen makes you feel. We just want staff to become aware, so that if their buttons are being pushed another staff can take over or they can work it out. And we have very strong support among the staff; we don't just care for the kids, we care for each other as well.

Another essential strategy Warming House staff employ is holding constant to a philosophy of accepting the young people for what they are. Although to an outsider the milieu and attitudes appear extremely stressful, the staff seem to have an almost Zen-like oblivion to the loud music, shouting, cursing, and fighting around them. One longtime staff member explained, "These are their norms for behavior: the clothes, the cursing, the music—they're not appropriate for other places, but we want them to feel comfortable here. Once you understand how they are, you don't take it personally." Rejecting these young people for their antisocial ways or insisting that they conform to standards of conduct would defeat the purpose of The Warming House. Teens come to The

Warming House because they feel accepted; the support and positive influences the Center offers are only available to them if they choose to come. In recognition of this higher purpose, the staff work to accept these young people at their own level.

Still, this philosophy presents conundrums. Smoking is an area of concern for the staff of The Warming House, as for many youth agencies. Most of the teens who frequent the Center smoke; although they are not allowed to smoke in the building, they can smoke outside. As one staff member explained:

> We can't forbid them to smoke around here, because for many of them it's such an addiction that they just wouldn't come. And we want them to come. But on the other hand many kids come here because it is a place to smoke, and so in that way we're promoting or encouraging it. They all know how I feel about smoking; I tell them every chance I get, . . . but it's a very hard thing to change.

Similarly, the harsh language and "in-your-face" behavior of many of the young people at The Warming House certainly dissuade others from coming, especially young women. Despite the fact that staff expressly criticize behavior that is abusive to young women, it remains an environment where, as one staffer said, "Only the toughest girls can hold their own here," and there are usually far fewer girls than boys in attendance.

The Warming House's philosophy of acceptance leads staff to focus on support and influence as a route to growth and development. As Adrienne Felder Mittelman, the current director of the Warming House, said:

> I think students come here and they try a lot of things on. And what we try to do is say, "I know you don't really believe the things you're saying sometimes . . . I know that's not really you, I know that you're trying that on, and you're asking if it's ok. You're showing something that you don't really understand." And what we try to do is to say, "let me help you understand that" . . . We try to see past the negative stuff they try to throw our way and say, "Wait a minute, I know there's gold underneath the surface, and we're going to sit with you through this process of uncovering that."

Indeed, the interactions between staff and teens can offer new options for behavior. "Some kids here act out to get a reaction from people," explained Laura Rodenkirch. "Here, we're trying to show them that they can get a reaction just by being themselves."

The staff of the Warming House seem to take these teens in stride, in part because they are not far from teens themselves. "When I first met the kids here,

I said to myself, 'Yeah, I remember what it was like to be a teenager: I was a jerk a lot of the time; I had a lot of free-flowing anger, too,' " said one staff member. Most are young enough to remember that they wished they'd had a place like The Warming House when they were growing up. The staff are also clearly empathic, energetic individuals. As Cindy Nash said,

> If you talk to our staff, a common thread is that everybody loves teenagers. That does not mean loving the perfect teenager but loving the teenage dilemmas, and the teenager persona—how hard it is, how vulnerable it is, how out of place you feel. Everybody can appreciate that struggle and how lonely and difficult it can be, and so we all have this empathy for them. But it is more than that. We love to see them in that struggle, because we know what's on the other side: no one can become a healthy adult without having had that struggle.

*   *   *

Care is not a free-floating, amorphous sentiment: it is bounded by the needs of the one cared for, the capabilities of the caregiver, and the circumstances of their relationship. This chapter will explore the many ways in which the practice of care is shaped by both the giver and the receiver of care, in an attempt to show how care is a mutual, interactive process defined by the circumstances of the relationship. The boundaries of the care relationship, the responsibilities of both parties, and the expectations for the relationship vary among different organized care settings. However, the essence of care, a practice that is mutual, self-generative, and contextually bound, remains constant.

As described in chapter 2, care involves the ongoing practice of three components—attentiveness, responsiveness, and competence—that continually interact. Care is an interactive process in that both the caregiver and the person being cared for contribute to the relationship. Mutual engagement on some level is essential to the practice of care. If one party disengages from the relationship, care cannot continue. This feature of care distinguishes it from service provision, as well as from the unconditional, unidirectional relationship of a parent and a child.

Care is also self-generative, both because its inherent mutuality requires the care recipient to care as well, and because the capacities necessary to become a caring person are nurtured by the experience of being cared for. The work of Erik Erikson and other developmentalists presents trust as the primary building block of all social capacities. Trust is foundational to caring in all relationships because of its essential role in the development of capacities to care. In this chapter, trust is considered as foundational to personal capacities and interpersonal relationships; later chapters will explore how trust is essential to caring organizations and large social systems.

Caring is powerful and consuming work, and boundaries must be established to protect caregivers and recipients alike. Boundaries and guidelines demonstrate to parents that those caring for their children are competent and trustworthy. Boundaries also allow care providers to husband and leverage their ability to provide care. An important means of husbanding care is by setting reasonable expectations for the care relationship. In particular, it is essential to see care not as the direct agent of change, but as the context in which growth and change can occur.

THE MUTUALITY OF CARING

The previous chapter described care as an endlessly cycling process in which attentiveness to the care recipient's response to care, as well as to his original needs, is essential. In this interactive process, the one cared for is not merely an object, but very much a subject. Although the process of attentiveness, responsiveness, and competence describes caring from the caregiver's perspective, it assumes the active presence of an object of care who is engaged in a process of her own.[1] The educator and philosopher Nel Noddings has described the many ways in which the object of one's care influences the caring process.[2] The one cared for may be more or less receptive to the care. She may be more inclined to strive to meet the carer as an equal, or more comfortable in the role of child, student, or acolyte. She may be more or less capable of responding to the care, and more or less attractive to the carer.

Thinking about care as a process of action, reaction, and renewed action highlights the relationship between carer and cared-for. Caring actions happen not only in the context of particular needs and circumstances, but in the context of previous actions, responses, and reactions. Both the giver and the receiver of care are party to this relationship; although the giver may contribute far more to it, both are essential to its success. Though the care relationship is not necessarily equal, it must be mutual.

Mutuality is not the same as reciprocity. Mutuality does not require the one cared for to respond in kind. It refers to the care recipient's response to the caring behavior of the carer. It can be as simple as acknowledgment or appreciation; it can also be expressed in demonstration of positive effects of the caregiver's actions. For a teacher, for example, mutuality might involve learning and growth on the part of the student. The cared-for's ability to respond in some form is essential to the caring process. There are many care relationships, however, in which reciprocity is not present.

As children enter adolescence, it is only natural that those who care for them expect them to contribute more to the care relationship. Care conceptualized along the lines of maternal care, in which a mother strives to meet her child's every need without regard to the child's contribution to the relationship, offers a picture of a unidirectional relationship. While infants and children clearly influence the caring process, they are not responsible for it. In contrast, the care offered by adults in organizations relies, in part, on the young person's willingness to take on some responsibility in the relationship. The young person must reciprocate on some level by "caring for" the organization. This expectation is still not reciprocity: those that provide care for the young person have no expectation of receiving similar care in return. It is a requirement that the young person be willing to engage in the social organization on its terms and to become a part of a group in which the needs of others, in addition to his or her own, are given consideration.

At The Warming House, as at other voluntary organized care providers, a young person takes responsibility for the relationship in two basic ways: by showing up, and by adhering to the organization's rules and expectations. All organizations set some boundaries that define unacceptable behavior and set standards for engagement with the organization. These kinds of limits for young people are both essential to an organization's viability and necessary to a young person's development. Beyond offering young people guidelines for current and future relationships, standards of behavior help to nurture the mutual engagement and responsibility necessary for successful adult interactions.

The conditions of participation at a place like The Warming House are an integral part of the caring the Center provides. Setting expectations and helping young people understand the consequences of not meeting them is an important part of care because it establishes mutuality. "Some of the young people with whom we've worked have parents who have given them so much, but have never said, 'No, this is unacceptable,' " said Cindy Nash of The Warming House. "They are looking for someone to set boundaries for them, and we would be letting them down if we didn't hold them to the rules." In this respect, failure in an organized care situation can be a constructive process. Exposure to a situation in which there are standards for behavior and expectations of mutual responsibility offers young people a benchmark for adult relationships.

Showing care by setting limits for young people distinguishes providers of real mediated care from programs designed merely as entertainment or diversion or to control behavior. Holding young people to high expectations of how they are to treat themselves and others offers opportunity for growth, both by establishing standards for future relationships and by offering young people real choices in their actions. In contrast, programs designed as means of controlling youths—to keep them off the streets or away from places where they might disturb adults, for example—are likely to be far less concerned with young peoples' investment in, and benefit from, the demands of an organization.[3] Mutuality also distinguishes care from service provision. A young person in an organized care relationship is not a client: she is an active participant in a relationship that cannot exist without her investment and efforts.

TRUST: THE FOUNDATION OF CARE

The importance of the relationship between the carer and the cared-for illustrates the ways in which caring is self-generative. Part of caring for the other is enabling the other to care for himself and for others who might be in need.

Trust is also important to establishing what one researcher has called a "sense of attachment to others and feeling of responsibility for the welfare of others."[4] This orientation to the world leads one to a habit of action, of responsiveness and attentiveness to others that constitutes the inclination to care. Most researchers speculate that such "sustained habits of orientation to the world"[5] are developed early in life.

The notion of trust as foundational to interpersonal social engagement is the hallmark of the relational, or psychosocial, approach to development advanced by Erik Erikson and Hans Kohut, among others. In his books, *Childhood and Society*; *Identity: Youth and Crisis*; and *The Life Cycle Completed: A Review*, Erikson presented an eight-stage life cycle, in which new abilities emerge from the successful application of the capabilities developed in earlier stages to age-appropriate tasks. Erikson stressed the importance of relationships, and particularly the child's primary relationship with his caregiver, to the development of individual strengths and capacities to engage in future relationships. The "task" of infancy, according to Erikson's theory, involves developing trust in one's caregivers and in one's own body and urges. With consistent, responsive, appropriate care (construed by Erikson as primarily maternal care), an infant learns to view the world as predictable and reliable, and to value his own feelings and impulses. He learns that the world is worthy of engagement and that he is worthy of engaging in it.[6]

Since Erikson's seminal theoretical work, numerous psychologists have tried to understand the mechanisms involved in positive social development throughout the life cycle. A foundation of this research is attachment theory, developed by John Bowlby and, subsequently, Mary Ainsworth to conceptualize how a child's first relationship affects development. Attachment theory posits that an infant's responsive, secure relationship with her primary caregiver, usually her mother, forms the basis of her own self-image, which the infant carries with her to all future relationships. Children who are securely attached have learned to trust that their caregivers will respond appropriately and consistently to their needs, and have developed an image of themselves as worthy of this kind of care. In contrast, children who have experienced inadequate care, inconsistent care, or care that is often detached or overbearing, may come to adapt by developing, in Ainsworth's terms, an anxious or resistant relationship with their primary caregiver. Moreover, attachment theory posits that such children will also develop a "working model of self" as someone who is unworthy of appropriate care. Researchers have developed reliable empirical measures of attachment, and longitudinal studies have explored the connections between the quality of the mother/child attachment relationship and young children's sociability, emotional maturity, and success in school.[7]

The personality characteristics of securely attached children— sociability, emotional expressiveness, and self-esteem—appear to be strongly related to a tendency toward prosocial behavior. Gregarious children engage in more prosocial behavior than shyer children; it is possible that outgoing children might do so in order to initiate social interaction, while more introverted children choose not to help in order to avoid social interaction or attention. Assertive, self-confident children are more likely to approach other people spontaneously and offer help, and are more likely to share possessions without being asked.[8]

In this light, trust can be seen as the foundation of a healthy and engaged personality. Speaking in Erikson's terms, it is the primary necessary component of social development upon which all future capacities are built. Trust allows the toddler to develop independence by experimenting with external objects and his own physical self. It is crucial to developing initiative and industry in early and middle childhood and to forging an identity in adolescence. The capacity for trust allows the young adult to engage in intimate relationships that require giving, constancy, and sacrifice. Finally, trust, along with the strengths developed in later stages, is essential for the central task of adulthood, care.

Not surprisingly, the capacity to trust also makes some young people more adept at developing supportive relationships with organized care providers. Young people differ in their capacity for mutuality in care relationships, especially at the beginning of a relationship. Those that have had positive experiences in intimate relationships are more likely to approach a relationship with an organized care provider with a presumption of trust. They will be more open to the trust-building process that is foundational to any relationship. In contrast, young people who do not have experience with trust will likely have a far more difficult time engaging in the mutuality necessary for a caring relationship. It might take significantly longer for that person to feel at all responsible for the relationship, or cultivating such a level of engagement might be impossible. Such youths require far greater up-front investment by an organized care provider; yet in many cases, it is these youths who have the most to gain in a successful care relationship.

There is a final and, perhaps for adolescents, most important, means by which care begets caring. In relationships between caring adults and adolescents, the caring adult becomes a role model and caring a valued trait. This is true both because caring becomes identified with a positive influence and because caring adults implicitly and explicitly transmit values about caring. In his essay *On Caring*, Milton Mayeroff explains this process: "People who care value caring in others and tend to encourage it and further it in others."[9] As one young man at The Warming House explained,

> The way that we are treated here is definitely the way I want to treat people. We are treated very nicely, they are very respectful; we are not like little kids here . . . It is not even that they are teaching us; it is the way that they are.

BOUNDARIES: PROTECTING YOUTHS AND PROTECTING CAREGIVERS

In its idealized form, care is always beneficial and in infinite supply. But in practice, every relationship is limited by the circumstances of the relationship, the ability and commitment of the one cared for to enter into the care relationship, and the resources of the caregiver. It is also possible for irresponsible caregivers to misuse the trust young people grant them. Boundaries in care relationships can protect caregivers and youths alike from relationships that consume an inappropriate amount of time or attention or unwittingly support destructive behavior. Boundaries also serve as indicators that an organized care provider will use its influence responsibly.

Philosophical inquiry into caring has generally focused on an intense, idealized form of care. The philosopher Martin Buber offered such a vision of care in his description of I-Thou relations and the I-Thou relationship, which he characterized by directness, or genuine rapport, openness and receptivity to the other, mutuality and reciprocity. Another important feature of I-Thou relationships is the total involvement of both parties. The participants must not attempt to hold back any part of themselves; their whole beings must be involved.[10]

Care has also received a great deal of attention in recent feminist philosophy. Many feminist writers have attempted to use the mother/infant relationship as the model for the caring relationship, in the context of referring to a maternal motivator for care that forms the basis of much feminist theory on care. The philosopher and educator Nel Noddings describes an ethic of care as "characteristically and essentially feminine" and asserts that caring is a nonrational process: "I do not feel that taking care of my own child is 'moral,' but, rather, natural."[11]

These descriptions pose several problems for thinking about care for youths in professional settings. First, the commitment described in these relationships is by its intensity limited either to a brief moment of time, or to a very few relationships, or both. Buber writes of the fragility of the I-Thou relationship. "Two friends, two lovers must . . . experience ever and again how the I-Thou is succeeded by an I-He or I-She."[12] Second, such care is not accessible to everyone. The mother-infant relationship is unique in the relative inequities of competence, motivation, and responsibility. It is probably not a good template for relationships in which more mutuality is possible, and even desirable. Finally, the idealized dyads of intense care limit care to a one-to-one, consuming relationship. This kind of relationship is probably not the healthiest or safest relationship for a young person.

As seekers of care, young people are vulnerable in relationships. Responsible caregivers understand that adolescents are often not developmentally capable of protecting themselves. The energy and enthusiasm that they bring to activities to which they are committed leave them vulnerable to exploitation. Their intensity of their feelings strengthens the influence of those in whom they place their trust.

Articulated terms and boundaries among caregivers can help parents and young people distinguish between caring programs and those few that might exploit or harm youths. Some boundaries are obvious: for example, prohibition of intimate relationships between adults and youths, or limitations on engagement in political or fundraising activities. Others are more subtle: an organization might set restrictions on when and where staff and youth may interact, or might have codes of dress, behavior, or address that reinforce healthy boundaries between adults and youths. The presence of guidelines for relationships indicates that the organized care provider understands the power of these relationships and the necessity of ensuring that they are uniformly supportive and facilitative of development.

In organized care situations, practical considerations make limits to care essential. In practice, no one individual is caring all the time, and no program can meet all the needs of its participants all of the time. Choosing when and how not to care is an integral part of the caring process. Boundaries in relationships also indicate the presence of a professional, well-trained staff that understands the developmental needs and capacities of adolescents. Staff with realistic expectations of the needs of their charges are less likely to become frustrated and "burn out." Well-run organizations have also developed specific limits on young people's behavior that protect both staff and other young people. Setting limits for young people is one way of protecting, and thereby sustaining, an organization's ability to care for many.

Organizations can be efficient care providers because they can both support and husband individual caregiving abilities. The structure of an organization helps to limit any individual's exposure to the needs of care recipients. Multiple caregivers allow for a sharing of burden. Different programs, activities, and staff offer a variety of options to reach different youths. And the continuity of the institution itself means that a young person attaches to, and relies on, more than a single individual.[13]

Perhaps the most important way in which caring individuals and organizations husband their caring potential is by holding realistic expectations of what they can accomplish. Some young people do not want to be reached; others have problems of such a magnitude that no single person or organization can make enough of a difference. Even in the best situations, change is slow and incremental, and depends more on the young person than the adult. Experienced youth workers understand that they can be positive influences in young people's lives, but they cannot effect change directly. Although there are many troubled youths at The Warming House, the staff understand that they cannot change these teens' lives. Change will come only when the young person wants it. "None of us here feel like we are here to save them," said Lynice, a staff member. "We want to help them find answers."

CARE AS THE CONTEXT FOR CHANGE AND GROWTH

Rather than viewing care as a mechanism for promoting development, care can be considered as a necessary *context* in which growth and change can occur. The difference between a mechanism and a context is that the former effects actions while the latter merely promotes or inhibits actions on the part of another—in this case, the young person himself. If we see care as a context, we recognize that growing, changing, developing are things that a young person does herself, with (one hopes) the support, guidance, and influence of caring adults. Caring relationships do not change people, but allow them to change themselves.

Caring is action and yet not a mechanism: caregiving activities are directed at another but not performed on him. Care meets needs, but development does not occur as a direct result: it occurs in a context in which needs have been met. Care provides safety, security, and most of all trust: thus it facilitates and supports development. Safety becomes the medium in which real relationships with role models can develop and personal growth, with its failures and humiliations, can occur.

This, of course, is what mutuality in care really means: the caregiver demonstrates attentiveness, responsiveness, and competence to the one cared for, and the one cared for responds by changing, growing, becoming more capable or mature, developing new capacities. As one staff member of The Warming House explained:

At first you feel like "I can intervene and do something and really affect their lives" and then over and over you learn that it is really not your job to intervene directly; really it is my job to give them opportunities to intervene for themselves, to change themselves.

CHAPTER 4

LEARNING TO CARE

Germaine's tiny blue house on 72nd street in southeast Kansas City looks barely more than one room square. Sitting on an overgrown lot, covered with an oddly shaped, red tarpaper roof, the house almost seems in danger of tipping over. Yet some afternoons it is safe haven to more than 25 children between the ages of 6 and 14, who call Germaine, 19, their "Block Brother." A program developed by the Boys and Girls Club of Greater Kansas City, Block Brothers employs young men between the ages of 16 and 19 to serve as role models, mentors, big brothers, and best friends to elementary and middle school children in their immediate neighborhoods. The Block Brothers take their charges to the local park for pickup football games, on field trips, to the library, to hang out at the mall. They visit the children in their group at school, watch them perform in plays and sporting events, and help them with their homework. Most of all, the Block Brothers make themselves available to the children in their group at all hours, every day, and encourage the children to spend time with them at their houses on weekends, afternoons, and evenings.

The Block Brothers program was founded as an alternative to the traditional "up and out" intervention programs of the inner city. "Most intervention programs are concerned with raising the individual up, helping him to get an education and stay off the streets, and taking him out of the environment he's from," explained John Brooks, director of operations for the Boys and Girls Clubs of Greater Kansas City. "That's fine; but we wanted to develop young men—young men in particular because there are so few successful African American male role models in the inner city—who would be successes and would be leaders in their community, young men who would understand the value and importance of giving back to their community." The Block Brothers Program is distinctive in its effect on the young men who staff the program. Being a Block Brother is a job, but it is also a carefully managed developmental experience.

The Kansas City program is small—only eight or twelve Block Brothers are hired at any time—and intensive. Nate Smith, the Block Brothers director from 1994 to 1997, recruits the young men from the working-class and lower-income neighborhoods of southeast Kansas City. "Basically, I beat the streets, talking to school guidance counselors, churches, and community groups, looking for kids who can be leaders," Nate explained. Nate interviews both the young men and their parents and makes sure the young men understand the responsibility they need to take on. After they're hired, each Block Brother is expected to recruit his own group of young people within a five-block area of his house.

Nate, a former Block Brother himself, serves as mentor and role model to the Block Brothers just as they do to their charges. "Nate is like a big Block Brother to us . . . we all know that if we have a problem we can go to Nate," said Germaine. It is Nate who tells them, when the pressures of juggling the demands of high school, extracurricular activities, and caring for a group of children begin to overwhelm them, "to kick back, forget about the kids for an afternoon. I'll take them out to a Royals game, just the Brothers," said Nate. "But then, wouldn't you know it, one of them will bring a few of his kids along anyway."

Nate assigns the Brothers biweekly writing assignments on current events and social issues, runs weekly meetings to plan schedules and monitor group activity, and hounds the Brothers about their handwriting and punctuation on the paperwork required to keep track of their charges. He models the intense commitment expected of the Brothers, and frequently finds they join him in volunteering for special events in the community.

Germaine has had to make his own way in life: his brother has had troubles, his mother has been ill, and she's had a series of abusive boyfriends living with them. Block Brothers, he said, "has been the best thing that's ever happened to me." In the three years that he's been a Block Brother, Germaine feels he's learned a lot. "I'm more considerate of people's feelings . . . I listen more, and think about how the other person feels." Germaine is clearly proud of the role he plays in his charges' lives, and of the success with which he's met the challenge to be a leader that the Block Brothers Program has offered. His pride is without bluster; he speaks with the self-confidence of someone who's used to being listened to, of someone who knows he knows what he's talking about. Nate Smith confirms that Germaine has matured considerably in his three years: he's become more patient, cleaned up a habit of cussing, and applied himself to school and a future in youth work. Germaine has entered a local community college and wants work for the Boys and Girls Clubs full time when he graduates. Most important, Germaine feels he's part of a family. "These guys," he said, pointing at some of the other Block Brothers, "they look out for me, and we take care of each other."

Each Block Brother receives extensive training at the beginning of his tenure in strategies for working with children, but it is the support network of Nate and other Block Brothers that provides them with grounding and perspective in their role. The peer group seems to be extremely important to these young men: when each one talked about his experience, he almost always said, "we" and rarely "I." The Block Brothers meet every Saturday to plan events for the week and to talk about challenges they're facing with children in their group. These meetings, along with the cookouts, sleepovers, and outings that Nate organizes for his Block Brothers, are times to share frustrations, solicit and offer advice, and feel as though "we are all a big family . . . we can all count on each other," as one Block Brother said. The Block Brothers help each other out with chores and money; they refer children who are interested in a Block Brother's particular skill to each other; and they very publicly back each other up in dealings with their charges. As one Block Brother said: "Yeah, you know all my kids know [the other Block Brothers]. They know that whatever [the other Block Brothers] said goes, they can't come ask me for something when Mike already said no. And we try to make it so they know we will all be there for each other."

Carl doesn't live far from Germaine, but his life has been a lot easier. The youngest child of a close family, Carl has an appealing softness about him— despite his 6'4" height—that shows he's been given a lot of love. He has grown up in a two-parent family with a father who's always been employed, and there's always been enough to go around. Carl's been lucky, and he seems to know it: he knows plenty of kids who don't have what he's had. As a Block Brother, he's learning to give back. "I was the youngest of three kids, so I always wanted a little brother," said Carl. "And these kids help me—they teach me responsibility."

"Carl used to be kind of stuck up, very into himself," reported Nate Smith. "He was very focused on who he was, where he came from. You don't see that so much anymore." A junior in high school, this lanky track star wants to become a kindergarten teacher. "People always laugh when I say that," he said. "But it makes sense to me. There are not that many black male teachers in the world, not that many men at all."

Carl juggles schoolwork, track practice, and responsibility for his Block Brothers group. Despite his schedule, he tries to see members of his group every day, and to spend quality time with each a few times a week. Some days he doesn't have time to be with them until 5:00, so they'll all come over to do homework together. Or he'll order a pizza on a weekend night and invite his group for a sleepover. "Basically, whenever I'm not at school or at practice, I'm with my kids," said Carl.

Nate likes to select Block Brothers who are active in school and community activities, but he admits the pressure on them can be enormous. Nate and John Brooks describe their biggest challenge as balancing the commitment and responsibility that the Block Brothers position requires with the other demands on these young men's lives. John Brooks explained the problem:

> You get a great kid and he is sharp, clean cut, intelligent, leader on the debate team, involved with a church, on a sports team, so you have everybody pulling on the individual and he is in the years of his life that you don't want to deprive him of anything, but how do you as a director say that he needs to do this, his kids need him . . . and you have Block Brothers feeling guilty because they feel like they don't have time for their kids after basketball practice, so as a director you need to be sensitive to all the demands and let them make decisions at some point.

These pressures are only compounded by the tremendous needs of many of the young people with whom the Block Brothers work. Germaine let out a burst of air and shook his head as he described the situation in his group this year:

> I had these two kids, the ones whose parents had died of AIDS. So I am dealing with them, making sure their heads [are] on straight so that they can then help their brothers and sisters. I had two kids whose parents died, one's father had a heart attack, and the other had his head shot off. And Mario, one of our kids, was in a car and three or four of the people in the car died in an accident and he lived. All the kids that these things happened to, they were all in my group and sometimes it makes you think that you should give it up, a lot of problems building up on you, and school work, and everything. But then when you look in the kids' faces and you know that they trust, you just can't turn away.

And indeed, these young men seem energized by their responsibility and encouraged by the small impact they can have on a child's life. When the Block Brothers talk about their work, they use such terms as role model, support system, and big brother, but what comes through is how much they enjoy building relationships with the boys and girls in their group. "I love having the kids come over—that's probably why I work so many hours, even without pay," said one Block Brother. It is the caring that excites them; and the Block Brothers

Program is a vivid demonstration that caring has a potent effect on the caregiver as well as the recipient.

Even with all the Block Brothers' hard work, the program's long-term effects on the children it serves are small in aggregate, if they can be measured at all. However, the impact on the Block Brothers is significant. "Even if you don't think you have it in you, you are forced to be a leader and make decisions," explained Nate Smith. "But I try to counsel them not to expect too much, that some expectations are not realistic." The young men who serve as Block Brothers are learning that leadership is not about glory and accolades, but about hard work, sacrifice, and failure. They are proud of themselves, but their self-esteem comes not from being told how well they are doing, but from seeing that their hard work makes some small difference.

Asked what the Block Brothers learn, Nate Smith replied, "Humility. I tell them all the time, humble yourselves." It is a different message than that usually preached to young African-American men in the inner city, but it is emblematic of a philosophy that values caring for others as an essential component of successful development. The program aims to teach these young men both what it takes to make a difference, and how valuable relationships can be. "I think that most of the Block Brothers would have done well without the Block Brothers Program: all of them won't go to college, some will go to the Army, some to trade schools, but they would all do all right," said John Brooks. "But the Block Brothers Program has helped them become even better. It has helped them feel compassion for the community."

*   *   *

One modern philosopher has described caring as "the disposition to respond to others and the world as worthy of engagement."[1] Caring is a habit of mind as well as of action, and like all habits it is most resolutely learned early in life. Like other aspects of character, caring is cultivated through instruction and experience in the context of an individual's capacities. How can caring be taught? Why are some people more caring than others?

In *The Altruistic Personality*, a study of Christians who rescued Jews from the Holocaust, Samuel and Pearl Oliner identified what they believed was the distinctive difference between rescuers and those who chose not to help others. In their view, the rescuers possessed what the Oliners describe as a heightened capacity for extensive relationships, "their stronger sense of attachment to others and their feeling of responsibility for the welfare of others, including those outside their immediate familiar or communal circles."[2] The ability and inclination of some individuals to transcend the calls of self-interest despite the extremely dangerous and uncomfortable conditions of wartime Europe was based, in the Oliners' view, on "sustained habits of orientation to the world, largely developed early in life."[3]

Previous chapters described how the capacity to care is rooted in trust in oneself and in the stability and predictability of the outside world. Trust has been described as the natural consequence of a secure attachment relationship in infancy.[4] But habits of caring are not entirely self-generated or dependent on early relationships. While caring has its roots in trust, it is cultivated through expectations and experience. It is a product both of being cared for and of being asked and expected to care for others. The experience of practicing care in family situations or in the larger community, as with service learning, has been shown to have a positive relationship with one's self-perception as a caring person and with future caring activities. Children who have assumed responsible chores in their families are more likely to think and act in prosocial terms as they mature.[5] Opportunities to care for younger siblings or relatives during childhood have been shown to enhance the development of empathic skills and caring behaviors.[6]

This chapter explains how caring is cultivated through expectations, exposure, and experience. Caring habits differ across cultures as well. Cross-cultural research has shown that children in subsistence economies are subject to vastly different expectations than those in more technically advanced societies.

This chapter also explores how the motivation to care develops in children and young adults. Older youths as well as young children are motivated by wanting to be like valued elders; adults are continually modeling behavior for youths. Finally, competence is a powerful motivator of caring, both by allowing one to expect that his efforts will be useful and by offering experience of the benefits of caregiving to the caregiver.

Since so much research in this area has focused on the role of the family, this chapter will concentrate on learning opportunities outside the family. Most of what we know about how youths become caring people is based on naturalistic observations of young people in family and community settings. We have little experience with interventions designed to promote caring. In other words, while we have a pretty good idea of the key factors in becoming a caring person, we don't really know whether those mechanisms can be successfully acted upon in program settings. We do know that circumstances affect individual development, and that many can identify specific turning points in life. We also know, however, that development generally follows a path characterized by continuity, not change.

Recently, youth community service, or service learning, has emerged as an intentional, institutionalized opportunity to "teach" caring. This chapter will review what is known about the impact of service learning experiences and discuss what these experiences can and cannot be expected to accomplish. Youth community service programs that exist in a context in which caring is not valued will likely have little effect. Young people need to have their direct experiences with caregiving reinforced by the culture of the institutions of which they are a part. In other words, teaching care requires that organizations become caring as well.

THE ROLE OF EXPECTATIONS AND SOCIAL NORMS

Caring—or "prosocial behavior," as it is academically termed—is not usually thought of as learned behavior, and most research into the development of morality and prosocial behavior is focused on the cognitive and affective dimensions of care rather than on such practical elements as skills or behaviors. The research literature stresses the processes of internalizing values and constructing personal standards more than developing a habit of care through practice and external expectations.[7]

The almost exclusive focus on motivations and internalizations in the development of caring behavior is not surprising when one considers the Western cultural and intellectual history of morality. The focus on individuals, on moral choices, and internally generated standards of right and wrong are constructs familiar to the Western philosophical tradition, and the development of care, like the development of all other social skills and values, is deeply influenced by culture. The structure, messages, and expectations of the culture determine, in great part, how and when caring is manifest in young people's behaviors. The normative ways of life in a culture determine the nature and extent of the opportunities to experience and develop competence in caregiving.

Children are adaptive creatures, and the kinds of people they become reflect the social and economic requirements of the culture and circumstances they inhabit. *Children become what their culture needs them and wants them to be.* It is of little value to compare cultures with the aim of determining "good" and "bad" childrearing practices: one can assume, taking a broad view, that childrearing practices have evolved to socialize the child in the manner most appropriate for the society in which he will take part.

What one learns about caring is in great part determined by the values and circumstances of the society in which one lives. Caring habits and skills are primarily passed along from parents to children, from generation to generation, as parents consciously and unconsciously convey messages about the child's responsibilities and roles in her environment through explicit instruction, expectations, modeling, and reinforcement. Such values are reinforced in the child's contact with other adults in her family and in the important institutions of her culture.

Cross-cultural research indicates strong associations between structural variables in a culture and values of cooperation, harmony, and prosocial behavior. In cultures in which there is a great deal of economic, social, and psychological interdependence, cooperation is often essential for survival. In planned communities with explicit ideologies of interdependence, such as intentional communes or the Israeli kibbutz, such cooperation is often highly institutionalized.[8] In some traditional cultures, values of cooperation and prosocial behavior are equally important but less intentionally reflected in the structure of everyday life. In many subsistence economies, for example, cooperation is essential for survival; and the childrearing strategies that promote a high degree of group participation and identification—such as communal living, being raised by a variety of caretakers and taught to share food and other goods—are a natural consequence of economic necessity.

One of the most famous and extensive cross-cultural studies of childrearing is Beatrice and John Whiting's Six Culture study, an examination of the everyday lives of children ages 3 to 11 in communities in Taira, in rural Japan; Tarong, in the Philippines; Khalapur, in northern India; Nyansongo, in western Kenya; a barrio in the Mexican state of Oaxaca; and a small New England town.[9] The Whitings and their researchers observed the household and economic activities in which these children lived and recorded the children's interactions with siblings, parents, and other relatives, as well as their play, chores, and other activities.

From this extraordinary study, the Whitings developed a theory that the degree of cooperation, prosocial behavior, and responsibility that children demonstrate is inversely related to the cultural complexity of the society in which they live. Cultural complexity includes such items as occupational specialization, a cash economy, primarily nuclear family living patterns, a centralized political and legal system, and a priesthood. The Whitings explained that the behavior of children in the six cultures they studied should be adaptive to the skills required in their cultures:

> Simpler societies, lacking superordinate authority, require a high degree of cooperation within the family, the extended family, the lineage, or the microcommunity. Complex societies, on the other hand, with a multiplicity of

roles and a hierarchical structure should train their children to be competitive and achievement-oriented.[10]

The Whitings found that the American community in their study ranked as the
most complex culture, and the children of that community were found to be
least nurturing, least responsible, and most dependent and dominant. The relative complexity of the other cultures also corresponded to the levels of nurturance, responsibility, and dependence observed in their children.

Experimental studies of cross-cultural differences in habits of cooperation
and prosocial behavior have also shown that children of more complex, urban,
individually oriented cultures tend to engage in competition even when it is
maladaptive to the task at hand.[11] Cooperation is not, of course, the same as
altruism.[12] Cooperation may be entirely self-serving or merely the most adaptive behavior. But to the extent that caring is a habit of mind and action, cultural norms that stress cooperation, of considering the collective as well as the
individual, and of practicing responsive, nurturing behavior might help one
develop the skills and values to become a caring person.

The Whitings concluded that prosocial behavior is developed by the experience and practice of care for younger relatives, assistance with household
chores, and other functions that contribute to the family's well-being. Caring
for younger children offers older children the opportunity to practice the prosocial behaviors that young children naturally elicit. When mothers are present,
they may also model and teach appropriate caring behavior.[13] Although the
Whitings and their colleagues conceded that children and adults are biologically
"prepared" to express nurturing behavior to babies and young children, they
stressed that it is the actual practice of care that develops an inclination and
capacity for prosocial behavior. Other researchers have also found associations
between being assigned caring tasks and developing caring behaviors. A study of
the Luo of Kenya demonstrated that boys, usually boys without older sisters,
who performed chores generally assigned to girls were more prosocial in their
overall behavior than their peers who did not have as much experience with traditionally feminine tasks.[14]

The Whitings also speculated that participation in chores, even tasks that
are not particularly nurturing such as gathering wood or water, gardening, and
cleaning and sweeping, enhances the development of prosocial behavior both
by training responsibility and by contributing to a sense of personal worth and
competence. In subsistence economies in which women's workloads are highest, children are assigned such chores as a matter of necessity. Children play an
important role in the maintenance of the family well-being, and their tasks are
essential and of benefit to the entire family unit. In contrast, in more Western-

ized, modern societies women's workloads are less burdensome, and the tasks that children are assigned, such as cleaning their rooms, are less clearly related to the economy or welfare of the family as a whole, and more solely for the benefit of the child. Children are encouraged to spend their time on schoolwork, an egoistic and competitive endeavor, but one which is adaptive to their culture's expectations of their adult roles.[15]

The Whitings presented their findings not as indictment of Western society, but as an explanation of how children develop the skills, values, and habits that are adaptive to their culture. They were careful to avoid value judgments in comparing cultures, and even more careful to avoid judging which culture is more altruistic than another. Their focus was not on children's motives for helping, but rather on the habit of care as part of a way of life. They studied the practice of care, not morality. Yet their findings suggest that the Kansas City Block Brothers may be having a greater impact than they realize as they embrace the ethic and the habit of caring for others.

THE ROLE OF INSTRUCTION, MODELING, AND COMPETENCE

Although empathic responses and caring behavior are natural social responses, the motivation to care—what our model calls responsiveness—is to a great extent nurtured by explicit training in prosocial behavior. It can be cultivated through explanations, specific directives, preaching, and attributions for behavior. Instruction can occur in planned experiences as well as in spontaneous interactions such as discipline and reactions to others' needs. In addition to working with their neighborhood groups, the Block Brothers run a mentoring program in halfway houses for juvenile delinquents and volunteer at the family courts. According to Nate Smith, these kinds of community service projects have a strong effect on most Block Brothers:

> It exposes them to kids that are in such a bad state that they understand how relationships are so important. It makes them think about their experiences and they look back and think about a person who was there for them and what that person meant, how special that person was, and how they can give that back.

Many organized care experiences explicitly use their interactions with young people as opportunities to demonstrate strategies of coping and caring for others. Experienced youth workers are deliberately modeling a nonadversarial, supportive style of interaction. One Block Brother, commenting on the necessity of diffusing tendencies toward violence and confrontation, described how he worked to show respect and tolerance to younger children who had issues with him. "We try to show them that . . . if you can talk it out with me and I'm older than you, then you can talk to someone your own age."

Each Block Brothers group starts out by working as a group to set ground rules and develop consequences for breaking them. "That way," explained a Block Brother, "I can say, 'you guys set the rules, so you have to deal with the consequences.'"

Young people learn by example when authority figures employ respect instead of power in their dealings with youths, subjecting themselves to the same standards as the young people with whom they work. Paul Van Horn of the National Indian Youth Leadership Project and Nate Smith of Block Brothers both remarked that they never ask their charges to do something they wouldn't do themselves. Asked how they know the NIYLP staff care for them, several seventh graders in Gallup chimed in. "They say please," "They don't yell at you," and "They don't talk down to you."

Preaching—the expression of clearly articulated values—is another instructional strategy that cannot be overlooked. Again, the Oliners' research on Holocaust rescuers offers compelling evidence. The Oliners found that although nonrescuers and rescuers recalled parental concerns with aspects of equity equally frequently, rescuers spoke significantly more often in terms and phrases characterizing care in describing the values they learned from their parents. Moreover, rescuers were also far more likely to emphasize that their parents had taught them to extend these values to all human beings.[16]

Attribution, the process of offering an individual reasons for his actions, is a means by which adults can assist a young person in internalizing a view of himself as a caring person. Attribution has been shown to be a powerful force in the development of intrinsic motivation, and has been shown to be effective in promoting a variety of desired behaviors in children.[17] "I tell my kids when you are in my group, we are all family, all related, regardless of whether I am there or not," explained Germaine. "And like with the family, since I have kids from the ages of 6 to 17, I have the older ones look out for the younger ones."

Modeling and instruction can induce young people to practice prosocial behaviors, which might help them to come to think of themselves as capable of caring actions in the future.[18] John Brooks, the founder of the Block Brothers, explained:

> . . . what we often run up against is capabilities, like they just don't know how to deal with the situations. Like sometimes, the Block Brothers will take

their kids somewhere and they themselves will want to enjoy it, but they have to be reminded that they are not there for themselves, it's for the kids . . . These guys are 16, 17, 18 years old and still learning—but that is where Nate comes in.

In chapter 2, competence was described as the ability to meet another's needs, a skill that could be taught and cultivated. In the Block Brothers program, young men are coached by the director and give guidance to each other to become more effective and capable caregivers. Competence in caring is an essential aspect of the practice of care, without which one has only concern and good intentions.

Competence can also be a *motivating* factor in caring; that is, one's perceived competence can contribute to one's inclination to engage in caring behaviors, and in the process, more finely tune one's caring responses. An individual's perceived, as well as actual, competence can serve to motivate helping behavior in several ways, according to the psychologist Elizabeth Midlarsky.[19] In one respect, competence functions as a form of self-esteem, by encouraging one to act in anticipation of success. Each situation in which help is required allows one the opportunity to make a conscious or unconscious estimation of the likelihood that one will be able to respond effectively to the demands of the situation. One's perceived competence will influence this calculation. Likewise, all helping behaviors require some effort, or cost, to the caregiver. If one is adept at recognizing the needs of others and responding to them, such costs might seem less onerous. One who is "in shape" for a task will find it less effort than one who is out of condition.

Perceived competence is a crucial aspect of a self-concept that is oriented toward care. A young person with experiences in caregiving can build an identity as a person committed to and capable of caring behaviors. A view of oneself as "someone who helps" is likely to become a self-reinforcing habit of response. In other words, one becomes a caring person, in part, by recognizing oneself as such. And a caring person is not simply one who means well, but one who effectively meets the needs of others.

Experienced carers also know that caring is very rewarding, and this too is a powerful motivator. As John Brooks said, speaking of the Block Brothers experience:

Heaven help him if he makes a real difference in some kid's life, if he feels like he's had a real impact! 'Cause then he's hooked: he knows he can help, and he's always going to want to try and try. And that's exactly where we want him to be.

CONTINUITY AND TURNING POINTS IN DEVELOPMENT

The psychiatrist Robert Coles has written of the limitations of social science theory, noting that such theories fail to acknowledge:

> the *circumstances* that make for such a difference in our lives, the accidents, the incidents that come along out of nowhere, it seems. *Fate* is the word other generations used, and *destiny*–but, of course, to accept what such words imply about this life takes matters out of the hands of those of us who want control, who want to be able to predict all, explain all.[20]

That there is something random about one's development into a caring person offers an entirely new wrinkle into the developmental inquiry. One's circumstances in life—the temperament one has been born with, the situation of one's family, and the encounters one experiences outside the family—are by their very nature random and unpredictable. Yet they can be shown empirically and anecdotally to be powerful contributors to the type of person one becomes. As with all aspects of development, we should expect circumstances and personal characteristics to play important roles in the development of caring individuals. There are multiple paths to caring, and caring people do not all have similar histories, similar motivations, or even similar ways of caring. Although early experiences are often critical, the ways in which people translate their losses and deprivations into constructive, positive attributes are varied and more difficult to predict.

In fact, empirical evidence of the continuity between early childhood experience and adult capacities is weak. A number of researchers have examined the connections between early socialization experiences in the family, particularly the attachment relationship, and ability to establish successful relationships in adulthood. A review of this research suggests that evidence for such continuity is tenuous and limited to certain types of individuals.[21] It appears that one's interpretation of one's childhood is a better indication of one's success as a caregiver in adulthood than one's actual experience. For example, women whose own mothers were depressed or otherwise unable to build attachment relationships with them as children were found to be competent caregivers when they acknowledged and could rationalize their mothers' shortcomings.[22] The experience of early childhood does not, it appears, dictate one's future capacity to care, in great part because a range of experiences later in life, particularly subsequent interpersonal relationships, can modify its effects. Many who experience adversity in upbringing develop supportive relationships in adulthood with a spouse or sibling that serve as both a model and a source of support for relationships with their children.[23]

Some researchers have examined the existence of "turning points" in life, most often occurring in adolescence and early adulthood. This concept has been especially useful in understanding the successes of some youths from disadvantaged or at-risk backgrounds. Relationships with caring individuals during adolescence are often significant turning points. While one should be wary of romanticizing such experiences, in some cases they can be practically lifesaving. Meaningful experiences in early adulthood, such as marriage to a supportive spouse, a relationship with a close friend, the birth of a first child, and an employment experience, can have transforming consequences.[24]

Such turning points do not always involve relationships with other individuals. For many people, connection to a private or organized religious practice provides continuity in the face of existing material and emotional challenges and meaning to goals for a new direction in life. One large longitudinal study found that conversion to a fundamentalist religion functioned as a turning point for a significant minority of the at-risk individuals with mental health problems.[25] Several researchers have found that military service has helped to move young men out of poverty throughout the twentieth century, presumably by offering them access to education, new responsibilities, and a structured setting in which to mature.[26]

Although some research has examined the impact of naturally occurring relationships and experiences over the course of subjects' lives, few studies have taken such a long view of the impact of intentional interventions or programs. More research is needed to understand how, and whether, at-risk youth can be protected over the long term by intentionally structured caring relationships. Moreover, the transforming effects of relationships in adolescence on healthy, "normal" youths have only been studied anecdotally and retrospectively.

For most young people, however, adolescence is less about turning points than about continuity in development. The modern Western concept of adolescence as a period of "stress and storm" has distinguished these years from childhood and adulthood, but has also diminished the importance of relatedness and connectedness to the adolescent experience.[27] Although adolescence is a period of profound change, it is not necessarily a time of radical separations or great turmoil. With respect to relationships, there is both great continuity in development from childhood to adulthood and constancy in the processes by which development occurs.

Recent scholarship in relational psychology has emphasized the constancy in developmental processes throughout the life cycle. In contrast to a traditional view of development as progressing from dependence to independence, relational psychology focuses on the need for others and for being needed at all points in life. The psychologists Robert Galatzer-Levy and Bertram Cohler, drawing on the work on Hans Kohut, call this perspective one of the "essential other," in which relationships with others support ongoing development throughout life.[28] This perspective recognizes that the need for care is not solely an experience of infancy, but rather a component of healthy psychological functioning at all ages. Emotional maturity is not equated with independence, but with harmonious interdependence of self and essential others. Personality is not fixed by early experience, but continually develops throughout life; and later relationships have the potential to be curative and restorative.

In contrast to a view of adolescence as a search for autonomy and independence, adolescence can be seen as a period of reorganization of relationships. Although the role and significance of certain relationships change during adolescence, the need for significant relational experiences still exists. Adolescents do separate their identities from their parents in important ways as they recognize their parents are not the ideal images of their childhood. In the best cases, a new, more equal relationship with parents gradually replaces the relationship of childhood. But a constant need for relationships draws the young person towards others, particularly peers, to replace these ideals.[29] Through their interaction with new "essential others," young people gradually discover and appropriate new ideals by which to live.

Viewing adolescence as a period of relationship building offers a way of understanding how peers and caring adults can be catalysts to the development of caring individuals. The power of peer influence, both positive and negative, has been widely discussed.[30] With respect to caring, peers function in several different ways. In his study of outstanding adolescents in Camden, New Jersey, the psychologist Daniel Hart found that many of the caring youths he interviewed were supported and encouraged in their caring actions by networks of like-minded adolescents. An important reason that these young people affiliated with church groups, youth agencies, and other youth-serving institutions was that these organizations gathered together caring youths who in turn provided each other with essential social and emotional support.[31]

The peer group is an essential part of the Block Brothers program, offering feedback and ideas on working with children, support, and companionship. Peer relationships are also opportunities to develop and enhance skills of caring. Friendships in middle childhood and adolescence can provide some of the first opportunities to care for others on an ongoing basis. Unlike relationships within the family, peer relationships are built upon an implicit understanding that each party shares responsibility for a shared trust and the maintenance of the relationship. Within that context, peers can practice the give and take that characterizes mutually supportive care. "I know if I ever have a problem I can call one of these guys . . . I know I can count on any one of them," said a Block Brother.

Of course, access to peer and adult relationships that foster and support the development of caring qualities in young people are as much a function of the individual youth as they are of the environment in which he exists. Some people are naturally more adept at attracting the help and interest of others and of engaging in ongoing relationships. From birth, some babies have "easy" temperaments, while others are more difficult to care for. Such individual differences confound any attempt to understand the impact of the "environment" as defined by relationship experiences. In their study of the life course of high-risk children, the psychologists Emmy Werner and Ruth Smith describe "a certain continuity" in the life course of successfully adapted individuals.[32] They found that the high-risk subjects who succeeded despite adversity had dispositions that "led them to select or construct environments that, in turn, reinforced and sustained their active, outgoing dispositions and rewarded their competencies."[33]

Caring is an interactive process in which cause and effect are not easily distinguished. It is tricky to talk about the role that relationships play in developing caring qualities when, in fact, the ability to engage in such relationships might be related to the ability to act in caring ways. Evidence of continuity in development in resilient youths who succeed despite discouraging odds and in young people who cannot be reached even by the most intensive, caring efforts offer caution to interventionists. We simply don't know how much we can accomplish through intentional caring experiences, and to what extent such efforts produce transforming changes as opposed to marginal ones. Much more research is needed to understand what is happening for young people in these experiences; we need to know more about how young people understand relationships with caring adults, how they integrate these experiences into their developing identities, and how these experiences relate to the overall context of their lives.

THE IMPACT OF YOUTH COMMUNITY SERVICE

If cross-cultural research such as the Whitings' Six Cultures Study have found that the experience of caring for others is an important part of becoming a caring person, it is perhaps only logical to try to expose young people in the United States to similar experiences. Recently, this effort has taken the form of organized community service programs with specific expectations for their participants. Politicians and community service advocates have been quick to embrace this type of service as a means of transmitting positive values to youth. Yet empirical evidence of the impact of youth community service is still scant.[34] Although they are intuitively appealing, community service projects are only beginning to receive in-depth evaluation to help understand their impact.

Many of the service learning programs now underway have been designed with broad goals in mind. A primary goal of many youth community service programs is the development of attitudes, behaviors, and competencies that will enable a young person to become a caring, responsible adult. It is hoped that by helping others young people will develop a habit of giving of themselves and increase their skills for communication, empathy, and cooperation.

Some of the most thorough recent examinations of the role of youth community service in promoting caring are contained in the ongoing work of Deborah Hecht, Joan Schine, and their colleagues at the Center for Advanced Study in Education at CUNY.[35] Their preliminary research findings suggest that students who have participated in service projects are less likely to respond to the problems of others with punishment, violence, or aversion, and more likely to solve problems through interpersonal communication than they were before their service experience, and than a control group of students who had not been involved in service projects.[36] Although student responses to hypothetical questions might not reflect their actual behaviors, changes in their responses after having service experiences does suggest that the service experience might allow the opportunity to develop more caring strategies for dealing with interpersonal problems. In a similar project with college students, researchers compared the written responses of participants in service programs with those of a control group when queried on a variety of social problems. Students involved in service learning programs showed significant increases in prosocial decision making compared to nonparticipants.[37] And a study of young urban adolescents randomly assigned to a school-sponsored program providing service in local health care agencies found that participating students reported that they engaged in fewer violent behaviors than a control group.[38]

Unfortunately, there has been almost no research on the impact of community service on caring behaviors. Hecht, Schine et. al found evidence that the effects of service learning might be very context-specific: adolescents who had served in a preschool were no more likely to respond with caring behaviors to scenarios concerning senior citizens than were their peers who had not been involved in community service. Little is known of the long-term effects of service experiences: researchers have generally studied the effects of caring experiences only at the end of specific programs. Although one longitudinal study found that young people who participated in school community service projects were more likely than nonparticipants to show extensive involvement in community organizations as adults, a review of the literature uncovered no follow-up studies to examine whether changes in attitudes or feelings persisted months, or even years, after the service experience.[39]

Another important goal of community service programs for youth is to provide them with an opportunity to assume a meaningful role in the extended community in which they live. Many sociologists, educators, and historians have written of the isolation and alienation of today's adolescents, who lack a productive role that has value and meaning to themselves and to those around them.[40] Proponents of youth community service assume that the experience of doing productive work to meet the real needs of others will make young people feel a greater sense of belonging in their communities and, therefore, increase their commitment and motivation to engage in society in a positive manner.

The results of research into changes in young people's attitudes about their responsibilities toward others and about people's responsibility to others in society at large have generally been mixed, with some researchers finding evidence of some changes and others finding none. When significant evidence of change is found, it is usually of a very small scale.[41]

Citizenship values are also widely assumed to be an important long-term effect of youth community service activities. However, available quantitative results demonstrate very little, if any, effect of community service experience on developing young peoples' sense of civic responsibility.[42]

Community service is seen as a venue in which young people can see that they can make a difference and an opportunity for youths to participate in "the real world." Advocates of community service for youth also hope that participation in meaningful, productive service to others will increase a young person's feelings of self-efficacy, and that these feelings will carry over into other aspects of the youth's life. The successful application of their energies to the needs of others will, it is assumed, increase their feelings of competence and their sense of the potential of their abilities. And indeed, one of the most consistent findings of research on the effects of youth community service is of increased feelings of self-esteem, personal adequacy, and self-efficacy.[43] Adolescents who have performed community service report greater feelings of competence in helping others after their experience.[44]

Findings of improved self-image among youths performing community service might result from the positive interpersonal contact many experience in community service work. Many students in programs under evaluation have indicated that the affection, respect, and appreciation from the children and adults they served were the most rewarding aspects of their experience.[45] Qualitative reports from interviews with participants have shown that the aspect of service programs young people most enjoy are "being with someone else" or with a group and knowing that they were doing something useful for others.[46]

Self-esteem might also flourish as young people acquire new skills and discover new talents. Tutors and child care volunteers learn how to work more effectively with children; youths working in community projects often report feeling more comfortable around adults. Exposure to the world of adults and work brings heightened feelings of competence and the knowledge that one can successfully take on responsibility. One Block Brother said: "We have gotten a lot of exposure, and we've had opportunities I never would have had if I hadn't been a Block Brother. Everywhere we go we meet people—famous and important people, people with tons of money—and they always remember us."

Impact on self-image, however, is highly contingent on the nature of the service experience. Young people who work in service roles that offer them the opportunity to develop relationships with others and to engage in helping others demonstrate greater satisfaction with their experience and show higher gains in measures of psychological development than those assigned tasks that involve less direct interactions.[47] Moreover, only meaningful involvement—defined by one researcher as "an activity that requires the active use of skills and which leads to a desired end—is positively related to self-esteem.[48]

Finally, many advocates of youth community service identify academic and intellectual outcomes as the most important goals for youths participating in such programs. School-related goals have gained prominence as the community service experience has increasingly fallen under school directorship. Service learning is seen as a form of experiential learning offering "hands-on" learning that is not available in the schools. Advocates of service learning claim that these kinds of experiences can enhance young people's development of problem-solving skills and critical thinking. Exposure to hands-on learning might foster a habit of lifelong learning, and might offer young people who have not been successful in school an alternative means of educating themselves. Moreover, exposure to situations in which knowledge and decision making are useful in real applications may motivate students to become more engaged in school, work harder at schoolwork, and reduce absenteeism. Finally, opportunities for youths to perform community service can provide exposure to possible future careers and role models and the opportunity to take part in the world of adults, vital preparation for the world of work.

Perhaps because so many of these programs have been designed and managed in school settings, the effects of performing community service on aca-

demic and personal outcomes have been somewhat more clearly demonstrated. Participation in service to others has been found to improve behaviors
consistent with academic success. Students involved in a community-based
learning or service experience have been shown to improve their attendance
records over comparison groups of students who are not involved, particularly
if participation is contingent upon attendance records.[49] Studies of the impact
of service learning experiences on youth-at-risk for dropping out and on
youths with disabilities, as well as on youths in general, have shown improvements in social behaviors in school and decreases in disciplinary problems.[50]

Gains in academic and cognitive skills have been found among students
involved in specific types of community service. Students who serve as peer
tutors or teachers of younger students have consistently been found to improve
in the subjects that they teach.[51] Moreover, service or other forms of experiential
learning oriented toward a specific topic area in conjunction with classwork has
consistently been shown to improve mastery and comprehension of the topic
relative to classroom-based instruction alone.[52] Participation in community service projects may also help young people develop more sophisticated thinking
skills, although the research in this area is by no means conclusive.[53] Evidence of
the impact of youth community service on attitudes toward learning has been
less directly studied, and the impact of service in this area is inconclusive.[54]

Finally, participation in youth community service does appear to have a
measurable impact on young people's attitudes toward and readiness for career
exploration. Exposure to and acceptance by the adult community appears to
encourage adolescents to anticipate and envision possible future adult roles.
Importantly, these effects have been found for community-based service experiences as well as for experiential learning designed to foster career exploration.
In many cases, service has offered insight into careers helping others.[55]

Programs like the Block Brothers offer inspiring anecdotes of how opportunities to care for others can help to instill values of service and interdependence. Yet a review of the research on caring produces mostly inconclusive
results. Why is evidence of service learning's effects hard to find in large studies? Some variability in findings of the impact of youth community service can
be tied to the varied nature of experiences to which the term refers. Not surprisingly, what a young person gets out of a service experience is highly dependent on what he or she puts into it, as well as on the quality of the service learning program.

But another reason for the scarcity of meaningful changes from service
experiences might be tied to the contexts in which many of these experiences
occur. The culture in which a service program operates offers as many lessons

as the program itself. Young people are learning not only from the structured program but from the behavior and values of the adults around them. If the messages inherent in the organization, procedures, and philosophy of a school, for example, are incongruous with the values of care that a service program seeks to instill, young people will have difficulty reconciling the incongruity, and cynicism about the program's goals may result. Attempting to teach caring while demonstrating practices and attitudes that do not value care might teach the dangerous lesson that care is a practice that can be compartmentalized and reserved for particular people and situations.

Caring can only be effectively "taught" if the lessons occur in a context that supports, models, and reinforces the desired behavior. Cross-cultural research suggests that it is the entire context of a young person's life that orients him or her towards prosocial behavior. The Block Brothers program has the impact it does because it occurs in a context in which young men both are expected to care and are cared for. The commitment, interdependence, and humility that is expected of them is modeled for them in a mentor, and reinforced in the context of a community-based, youth-serving organization. And it is from this context that the young Block Brothers try to help their charges see the world around them. As one Block Brother said,

> What they hear on the streets and in school is, you've gotta protect your own; don't worry about nobody else. We try to change that by letting them see that its good to have a friend that you can talk to and depend on. Regardless of what they see and hear, it can't just be you, you cannot do anything by yourself. Someone has to be there to help you.

CHAPTER 5

BUT WHAT DOES CARING "ACCOMPLISH"?

Hector Calderòn, a teacher at El Puente Academy for Peace and Justice in Brooklyn, New York, reflected on his first lesson as a teacher at this alternative public high school in a working-class Latino community:

> In '84 when I first got here, I thought that a lot of the learning had to be about how well I was trained in the discipline I was teaching. And I thought that's where it was at. That if I knew my material really well, then of course it would translate into having a good class, and what I realized, rather quickly, is that it was clear that unless I built relationships with young people, that no matter what I was teaching, that no matter how experienced I was, that that wouldn't be enough . . . Because at some point, you have to get the *permission* of young people to teach them. You can't just assume that because you have this title of teacher—and of course, they're used to the power relations between teachers and students— . . . that you will get to them right away . . . I just didn't understand that; I thought 'well, I'm young, I come from this community, I could relate' . . . but I realized that the only way I could get permission was through being truly involved in young people's lives . . . so that for every young person there, I had to be more that just a Global Studies facilitator. I needed to be Hector, a friend, Hector, a presence in their lives, somebody that cares about them, somebody that was there, building relationships in the service of learning.

Leon, a senior at the Academy, described the same process from a young person's point of view. "Kids like it when a teacher cares about them. They like it when a teacher goes out of their way . . . it makes them feel good, especially those who are more laid back, more quiet. They are not even comfortable with themselves and to see a teacher going out of their way to see how they are doing, that makes them feel good and that makes them open up."

"The principal barrier to caring on the part of agencies and so-called professionals who serve young people is categorization," explained Luis Garden Acosta, founder and executive director of El Puente. "Because once you go down the path of saying, 'I'm only here to prevent this person from being a dropout, or a pregnancy statistic' that's when you begin to discombobulate the individual. And then you can't really love—you don't see the person as a whole human being."

At El Puente, banners hanging from the ceiling emphasize the importance of body, mind, spirit, and community. Teachers, staff, and youth workers are all called "facilitators," to underscore the value of developing all aspects of the young people there. If it is difficult to tell the teachers and students apart, and the school curriculum from the community programs, that is by design. The point is to emphasize the entirety of the young person's life—her individuality of mind and spirit, her family, community, and culture—and to help young people develop identities that have meaning for and incorporate all aspects of their lives.

El Puente Academy for Peace and Justice is an unusual school: born out of a community center devoted to the social, political, and economic development of the Latino population of Williamsburg, it has been designed around themes of social justice and connection to community. El Puente Academy is one of the first Charter schools in New York City, schools created as independent, publicly funded alternatives to the traditional schools in the public school system. Students apply to El Puente in lieu of their neighborhood public schools. Founded in 1993, the Academy has won early praise for its success with students and the energy and commitment of its staff. As a community center, El Puente is in its seventeenth year and is justifiably hailed as one of the most successful community-based youth centers in the country. Its achievements in halting the environmental devastation of its community, reaching out to the large Hasidic, Polish, and African American communities with whom the Latino community coexist, and enhancing the cultural, social, and physical well-being of its community have been well documented. With its history of social activism and its focus on justice, El Puente offers insight into how caring social and political values, institutionalized in an organization, are expressed in "face-to-face" caring for young people.

What emerges from conversations with the staff and young people who populate El Puente is not a political ideology but a strong value system, a way of understanding life that offers young people both an acknowledgment of the entirety of their lives and a social context in which to construct their identities.

El Puente feels like a small village in which classrooms are but one venue for an ongoing effort to develop capable, connected young people. Young people and facilitators meet, visit, and talk in small groups throughout the extraordinarily small space that houses the school and community center, as well as in the homes, churches, and streets of the neighborhood. Teachers are expected to participate in the many special events and nonacademic activities as members of the extended El Puente community.

Although some students travel an hour and a half each way to attend El Puente, the school is designed to be rooted in and oriented toward its local surroundings. The school community extends beyond the walls of the school to neighborhood projects ranging from community gardens to a multiethnic alliance against industrial pollution. In all undertakings, the effort is to set the young person's experience in school within the larger context of the social, economic, and political life of a community. "We are trying to create a community in which it is repeated in so many ways that we are all responsible to each other—that our actions really have an effect on everybody," explained Frances Lucerna, the principal of El Puente Academy.

The school seeks to involve as many members as possible of the community—from the executive director's mother to local artists—in the lives of their students. The goal is to expose these young people to life models. "We hunger to find role models, adults whom we feel are images of success—not monetary success, personal success," said Luis Garden Acosta. Facilitators understand that their strongest method of teaching is by example. Many spoke of ways in which they tried to employ respect instead of power in their dealings with young people, subjecting themselves to the same standards as the young people with whom they work. Alfa Anderson, an English teacher at El Puente, described a time she was late for her own class:

> I have a rule that if you're more than five minutes late to my class you must come with a pass from the principal. This particular day I got caught up . . . and I got to class seven minutes late . . . I'm never late, but here I was late to my own class. And they [the students] said "You're late!" I said "I'm so sorry." And they said "Well, you need to bring a late pass." I could have pulled rank, and said no—I'm the teacher after all—but I decided it was the perfect opportunity for me to teach a lesson . . . When I got back they were very happy . . . I asked them, "What would have happened had I not gone for a pass?" They would have dealt with it, but they wouldn't have been satisfied; they would have been frustrated . . . they wanted to see that rules are for everyone, not just some.

The frequency of contact, the small number of students, and the shared values of holism forge an environment in which teachers feel responsible for knowing their students, and young people feel as though their elders genuinely care about them. This is attentiveness in practice. "They're on your case all the time . . . They care about your academics, but they also care about how you are . . . about other things that are happening in your life," said Joseph, a junior. "If you was to come with your face down, or whatever, they all ask 'So what's wrong with you? Are you all right? What's going on?' . . . The kids in my class know their teachers so well that they don't hesitate to speak about their problems."

Frances Lucerna described her daily morning ritual, in which she greets students in the front vestibule as they come in to school and tries to "check out" as many of them as she can.

> I do a thing every morning, and they all know it . . . I'm downstairs..: "So John, how's it going today?" . . . "So Louie" . . . "Hey Bobby, come over here . . . you don't look too good today—what's going on? What's up?" . . . I kind of feel these kids out.. It's kind of like being an open system, just being able to feel . . . where these young people are.

The ethic that mind, body, spirit, and community are connected leads every staff member to take responsibility for youth, and to see their responsibility in terms of all aspects of the young person's experience. "I'm not doing my job if I don't know what's going on for my student—at home, with respect to their adjustment to this culture, in their neighborhood," said Evelyn Erickson, a biology teacher at El Puente. Even the public relations director at El Puente has a mentor relationship with a group of young men who are students and members of El Puente. And El Puente refuses to have a social worker on staff, on the grounds that it is impossible to isolate "social work" from the rest of youth work.

"The dirty word here is 'agency,' " jokes Luis Garden Acosta. "The whole idea of 'agency' suggests that something is wrong with you and we are here to fix it. That is not what we need."

This focus on the whole person in the context of culture, community, family, and peer group supports young people's efforts to form identities that include social, spiritual, and civic values as well as academic and professional goals. "So many programs driven by academic success focus on bringing young people into the professional classes, as though the whole point was to become a doctor or a lawyer," said Luis Garden Acosta. "But for what? . . . Our focus is on what kind of person you become; what connections have you made to your community, to your spiritual life, to other people."

Caring for young people as whole individuals implies measuring success individually. "We don't care for conventional social science indicators; we're interested in how well a person has learned to create relationships with others, to express love and caring, to strive for mastery of all aspects of their lives," said Luis Garden Acosta. "Obviously, you have to know a person pretty well to know how he's grown in those ways." The end goals may vary, too, depending on the circumstances of the individual. "You have to look at the starting point for a particular individual," explained Acosta. "Is the one graduating from Harvard, who's had a pretty easy life, a greater success than the one struggling to graduate from high school in the face of family tragedy?"

Perhaps because the focus at El Puente is on individual goals and multifaceted indicators of success, students are held to high standards of behavior and engagement. Many appear to have flourished academically and personally under this combination of individual attention and high expectations. A great many people occupy an extremely small space at El Puente, yet one is constantly struck by how quiet these teens are, how respectful of each others' and adults' space they appear to be. A communal coat rack sits in the main hall: administrators have often reflected on what it would mean if staff and students came to be uncomfortable leaving their bags and possessions there, unguarded; but students seem to be equally sensitive to this barometer of trust, and there have been no thefts.

El Puente is clearly a rigorous environment, in which young people are asked to work hard and to ask hard questions. Frances Lucerna believes this environment is a direct result of the focus on caring: that despite popular misconceptions, caring and rigor are interrelated:

People think that once you talk about love and caring, especially in school situations, you are no longer talking about standards, about mastery, about rigor; that it's all touchy-feely. I really have a problem with that. That is *not* what this is about: if you really create a place where young people and adults come together and develop deep relationships of care, then mediocrity, getting over, failing, is irresponsible to oneself and to other people. We are very clear about that . . . There are tremendously high standards here, and a clear understanding of our responsibility to create the support for young people to achieve. If we don't give them the option and the support, it is very irresponsible and even criminal. This is really sacred work and this is a sacred place we have created.

*   *   *

Analyzing the role of being cared for in the healthy development of youth is inherently puzzling. Development is a process, not an event; and it is difficult, and sometimes counterproductive, to try to isolate the effects of one relationship or one experience from the multiplicity of influences on a young person's development. In fact, it is the interplay of a combination of influences that makes for healthy development.[1] The outcomes that one might posit to be affected by caring—such personal assets as educational commitment, social competencies, positive values, and positive identity—are similarly difficult to disentangle.[2] Attempting to do so defies an essential feature of their importance: the ways in which they act in concert to promote accomplishment and life success.

In the best circumstances care begets caring by helping individuals develop into people who can care for themselves and for others. The end goal of caring, to the extent that there is one, is directed toward the kind of person one hopes a youth will become. It is, therefore, positively oriented, focused not on problems or deficits but on healthy development and functioning. It is also holistic, considering the entirety of a person rather than specific attributes or accomplishments. Finally, caring is individually focused, both with respect to the actions and behaviors of care and to the responses and reactions of the one cared for.

But what, in the end, does caring really accomplish? Can we say with certainty that the relationships young people build with caring adults contribute to their healthy development and life success? How do we measure the impact of these relationships? How can we quantify the benefits of a caring classroom, a caring school, or a caring community?

In truth, we know very little about the effects of being cared for on young people's development. We can see evidence of neglect in self-destructive and sociopathic behaviors, as well as in depression, disengagement from school, and other failures. However, the research evidence of the effects of caring is still limited: very little research looks at caring directly, and few studies have extended long enough and covered large enough populations to be able to make strong claims. Almost all of the research in this area focuses on the role of caring relationships in the family; little quantitative research follows the impact of relationships with other adults. This chapter will survey what is known about the effects of being cared for on the development of young people. Most people believe that participation in positive relationships with caring adults contributes to positive developmental outcomes and prevents high-risk behavior; fewer can explain how or why. The aim of this chapter is to begin to develop an understanding of how such caring relationships can have an impact, and to consider how that impact can reasonably be demonstrated.

In recent years greater attention has been paid to the role of caring in creating positive school and classroom climates. The connections between positive social contexts and learning have been well established. Programs like the Comer Schools and the Child Development Project have demonstrated that large-scale environmental changes in a school, as well as classroom-level initiatives, can materially affect the academic outcomes of children. Most of this research centers on elementary schools; middle and high schools are seen as more complex and less malleable. However, research indicates that the factors contributing to a caring climate in elementary education are equally applicable to upper schools.

Caring is not a mechanism of development; it is probably more helpful to consider it as a context in which positive development can occur. This chapter will discuss caring's effects both as a protective factor in development and as a facilitating influence in learning, academic achievement, and the development of other skills. The distinctions between these concepts are not great, and relate primarily to the situation of the one cared for. Caring relationships provide support and guidance that can serve as a protective factor in the lives of young people in situations of stress or change. Caring relationships in classrooms and other settings can facilitate growth and learning by offering security and a sense of belonging in a challenging environment.

This chapter will also review the role that mentoring can play in the lives of young people. Mentor relationships are unique organized care programs in that caring relationships are their primary, stated purpose. Again, little is known of mentoring's long-term effects, but some recent research has shown how mentoring can be most effective.

Part of the problem in considering caring's effects on young people is that few have considered how caring can be measured. Where caring has been named as a focus of research, it is defined and measured in a non-standard fashion, referring sometimes to behaviors and sometimes to attitudes, and measured by peer and teacher nominations, self-reports, and a variety of questionnaires. The ambiguity surrounding the measurement of caring is particularly relevant as problems with measuring its impact hinder appreciation of its importance.

It may be, however, that it is not possible to measure caring accurately, or that even with useful measures the experiences of being cared for are too diverse and individual to be quantified across populations. Does this mean that caring itself is of no value? Or is there another way to evaluate and consider the impact of care? Could we take a leap of faith and accept that the process of care itself is of value, rather than ascribing its value to outcomes on which we assume but might not be able to prove care has impact?

CARE AS A PROTECTIVE FACTOR

The role of caring in promoting health and well-being, in supporting mental health, and in protecting young people from such high-risk behaviors as drug use, delinquency, sexual activity, and suicide has been examined from a number of vantage points. A great deal of research has considered the importance of *social supports* in enhancing physical and emotional health. Social support is a way of describing the network of personal relationships on which an individual relies for instrumental assistance, such as help with the chores of everyday living, material aid, information, and emotional support. It also encompasses one's social identity; that is, the group or groups by which one defines oneself. Social support involves relationships with one's family, friends, neighbors, and colleagues at work; it refers to both intimate affective relationships and more businesslike, instrumental relationships. Again, although this term is not synonymous with care, it can be thought to include behaviors and attitudes similar to those employed in the practice of care; specifically, the notion of ongoing, mutually beneficial relationships; the importance of attentiveness, responsiveness, and competence; and the relevance of circumstances.

Large-scale epidemiological studies have consistently found a strong association between social integration—frequency of contact with family, friends, neighbors, and co-workers—and physical well-being.[3] Health professionals have proposed that merely participating in interpersonal relationships is protection against stress and illness. From membership in a supportive social network—family, community, or other forms of mutual relationships—individuals derive a sense of stability, predictability, control, and the perception that others will help in the event of need.[4] These psychological states, social support theorists hypothesize, both affect behavior and improve immune system response. Socially integrated individuals are more likely to adopt health-promoting behaviors, such as proper diet and exercise and avoidance of alcohol and tobacco abuse. Feedback and guidance from others might also help individuals to avoid other life stressors that can impair psychological and physical health.[5] Finally, recent medical literature suggests that psychological well-being may itself improve immune system functioning.[6]

The strongest evidence of the causal effects of caring relationships on health is found in the connections between social connectedness and health-promoting behaviors. Adolescents who feel that they have strong supportive relationships within and outside their families have been found to have greater knowledge of health-promoting behaviors, have higher physical energy levels, are less likely to engage in unhealthy activities such as smoking or alcohol consumption, pay greater attention to health, and value physical well-being more that those who report less social support.[7]

The major health risks of adolescence, however, have less to do with prevention and health maintenance than with the avoidance of high-risk behaviors such as substance abuse, sexual activity, and deviance. Children raised in conditions of poverty, unstable or absent parenting, and other disruptions are at greater risk for these behaviors, both because of the stresses such conditions create in everyday life, and because these children may be more likely to lack relationships with caring others who can provide guidance and support during the challenges of development. Although the connections between these stresses and failures in development––such as high-risk behavior, mental illness, and poor health—are fairly well established, far less is known about how some children develop into healthy, competent adults despite growing up in stressful conditions. Recently, psychologists and health professionals have begun to focus on how at risk children might be protected against the stresses present in the organization and economics of their everyday lives. The term *resiliency* has come to indicate a mechanism of successful development. Instead of focusing on connections to problem behavior, research into resiliency considers the circumstances that might protect a child from the stressors of his environment. These *protective factors*—both personal qualities of an individual and circumstances to which he or she is exposed—serve as resources with which an individual can manage and diminish adverse situations that might otherwise lead to illness and problem behavior.

Recent large-scale research studies suggest that caring can play a protective function in development, buffering high-risk children and adolescents from the powerful social stresses present in their lives. One of the longest-running and most thorough of such studies is the Kauai Longitudinal Study, begun in 1955 by University of California psychologist Emmy Werner. Werner and her colleagues followed all 505 individuals who were born on the island of Kauai in 1955 for forty years, documenting the course of all lives from birth until adulthood. Their aim has been to understand the long-term consequences of perinatal complications and adverse rearing conditions on individuals' development and life experience. The researchers gathered information from the subjects' mothers during pregnancy, and interviewed the subjects at birth, infancy, early and middle childhood, late adolescence, and adulthood. From such a comprehensive study, Werner and her colleagues have learned much about the impact of medical complications at birth and stressful family environments on development. Most important, they have been able to identify several protective factors that can mitigate the effects of these biological and psychological risks.

Of the Kauai cohort, approximately two-thirds were born without complications, raised in supportive home environments, and experienced no unusually stressful life events. One in three, however, encountered several "risk factors:" they experienced moderate to severe stress at birth, grew up in chronic poverty, had parents who were alcoholics or mentally ill, or suffered parental divorce or desertion. Werner and her colleagues categorized children who were exposed to four or more such risk factors before the age of 2 as "vulnerable." Over the next two decades, they found that by age 18, two-thirds of these vulnerable children had developed serious learning, behavior, or mental health problems, had a record of delinquencies, or had become pregnant.[8]

While two-thirds of the vulnerable children developed problems as youths, one-third did not. A major contribution of the Kauai Longitudinal Study has been to document how children who were at risk for poor health and antisocial behavior "defied the odds" to become successful adults, capable of working, establishing intimate relationships, and participating in their communities. Werner and her colleagues found that high-risk youths who succeeded despite the problems they encountered were protected by individual qualities, family circumstances, and sources of support both within and outside their families. As infants, successful youths were rated as having an "easy" temperament and were described by their mothers as active, affectionate, and good natured. By age 10, resilient children scored significantly higher on measures of verbal comprehension, problem solving, and perceptual-motor skills. Family circumstances and birth order also played a part: successful youths were more likely to be first-born or, if male, to be the first son; they were also likely to have fewer siblings, but to have more adults living in their household, than youths who developed serious behavior problems.

The importance of social support and caring adults in protecting these vulnerable children was demonstrated most dramatically as Werner's subjects progressed from childhood to adolescence. Werner notes that while health service professionals were available to the Kauai cohort, only a small proportion of the resilient children and youths made use of them. Rather, resilient adolescents relied upon a number of informal sources of support, including peer friends, older friends (including friends' parents), parents, ministers, and teachers. High-risk youths with serious coping problems were found to turn less often to adults, whether parents, teachers, or friends of the family.

In a study of a subsample of the Kauai cohort consisting of children of alcoholics, Werner examined the role of caring adults and religious coping efforts in the lives of "resilient" adults.[9] These adults were interviewed as part of the final follow-up to the Kauai Longitudinal Study. Werner found that the individuals who had avoided serious coping problems as adults had been able to rely on a significantly larger number of sources of support in their youth. This support came both from within the family (for example, from the nonalcoholic parent) and, importantly, from adults outside the family. None of the men and only one woman among the offspring of alcoholics with coping problems in adulthood recalled receiving some support from a teacher. But about half of the "successful" adults encountered at least one teacher who became a positive role model. Resilient adults were also more likely to have drawn support from older friends and parents of friends than were adults with coping problems.

It is important to appreciate, however, that caring, like any other protective factor, is not an isolated influence that can be simply applied to a young person like a topical ointment. Rather, it is a complex series of interpersonal actions in which both the giver and receiver of care play a part. As discussed in the previous chapter, there is a great deal of continuity in the life course of resilient youths. Youths who are more socially competent are more likely to be able to elicit support from others, and more likely to be attractive to caring adults. These social skills are in turn reinforced and enhanced by adult expressions of care, leading such youths along a path of greater social support and stability. Young people who lack such resources are likely to have more difficulty attracting and engaging in supportive relationships with caring adults. Evidence that the availability of caring adults as sources of support is a crucial protective factor in adolescence suggests that many youths could benefit from more proactive efforts to connect them with such resources. If caring adults were more accessible, less socially competent youths might build relationships that they might not be able to initiate on their own.

The Kauai study highlights the importance of a wide network of available adults in coping with the changes of adolescence. Although parental relationships are generally the primary determiner of coping, the Kauai study, among others, demonstrates that relationships outside the family can augment the family support system or, in cases where parental influence is unavailable or negative, can offer supplementary, positive influences. As the primary occupation for young people, school plays an important role in shaping young people's self-image and in developing habits of interaction with work and community. Schools also serve as a significant source of caring adult relationships. Enjoyment of school and a feeling of belonging and connection to it—"school connectedness"—has been found to serve as the primary protective factor, even ahead of family connectedness, against acting-out behaviors such as drug use, pregnancy risk, delinquency, and unintentional injury, among both boys and girls ages 12 to 18. Among the same sample, school connectedness was second only to family connectedness as a protective factor against such quietly disturbed behaviors as suicide, emotional stress, and eating disorders.[10]

CARING IN THE CLASSROOM

A positive school experience is often a source of many of the caring relationships that promote positive physical and emotional development throughout adolescence. Caring can also be considered as a facilitator of successful experiences in school and in other arenas of young people's lives. Viewing caring in this way recognizes the influence of social contexts, including relationships, on thinking and learning. In contrast to the classical image of the child, in isolation, learning by experiment, a social cognitive approach considers the interactions by which individuals learn. This focus on social contexts considers the human relationships, cultural practices and expectations, and other qualitative aspects that shape the learning environment.[11]

The large body of research on school failure demonstrates the importance of young people feeling engaged in the social context of school. Disengagement with the purpose and meaning of school is increasingly recognized as the first step toward dropping out. In a recent review of the research on youths who drop out of school, disengagement was presented as a gradual process that develops when students do not feel a sense of belonging in their schools.[12] This review found that developing a sense of belonging and valuing school goals were the key factors in prevention efforts aimed at youths at risk for dropping out. Other studies have found connections between belonging and school values: students who report feelings of belonging and social support are found to hold higher academic values.[13]

Many educators and policy makers have questioned whether positive social factors such as engagement, self-efficacy, and motivation really affect academic achievement. Some have derided a focus on self-esteem and other "feel-good" initiatives as peripheral to learning and skill development. However, research has shown that children who are more engaged in school do earn higher grades and score higher on standardized achievement tests.[14] Children who are positively engaged in school certainly pursue activities that should lead to superior academic performance, as the following description suggests:

> Children who are engaged . . . select tasks at the border of their competencies, initiate action when given the opportunity, and exert intense effort and

concentration in the implementation of learning tasks; they show generally positive emotion during ongoing action, including enthusiasm, optimism, curiosity, and interest.[15]

Engaging students in the classroom is a highly individual process; every teacher has his or her favorite strategies. It is clear, however, that true engagement arises both from personal interactions and from the messages communicated by the teaching philosophy of school staff. Consistency to a core set of values focused on attentiveness, responsiveness, and competence most effectively reinforces the positive connections developed in face-to-face interactions. Creating a caring classroom involves both personal style and practices that communicate that these values undergird the purpose and mission of the classroom and the school itself.

Creating Positive, Nurturing Teacher-Student Relationships

Research across school grades has demonstrated that the quality of the teacher-student relationship is a critical determinant of student engagement and motivation. Emotional sharing and security with teachers are major predictors of student classroom engagement.[16] "The first element is creating a safe, nurturing learning environment," explained Alfa Anderson of El Puente, ". . . where it's okay to make mistakes, where it's okay to fail, where it's really okay to understand that success comes after failure."

Studies of the transition from elementary to middle school have found that junior high school students find their new teachers less supportive and more controlling than in elementary school, and that such changes in the quality of the teacher-student relationship are negatively associated with student motivation.[17] High school students who perceive their teachers and principals as caring persons have been found to report a higher sense of belonging, greater satisfaction with their school experience, and greater feelings of self-efficacy and academic ability.[18] Similarly, high school students who reported better interpersonal relationships with their teachers were found to have higher grades, to be absent from school less often, and to report that they more consistently did their homework.[19] Josh Thomases, a Social Studies and Humanities facilitator at El Puente, illustrated the day-to-day impact of caring relationships in the classroom:

You want to be able to establish the kind of trust that allows you to call on young people and demand that they be present in their work. To push them when they are struggling and say, "I know you can do this." And have that not come from some random voice, [so they say] "That's the teacher's voice," and put it away. But to hear from somebody who is really a part of their lives, so it might cause them to stop and think, "Oh, if they believe in me, ok, maybe I should believe in myself."

A responsive, friendly personal style sets a tone where positive relationships are possible. "It's simple things: if someone's absent one day, when they come back the next day I welcome them back to the class: 'I missed you yesterday! Is everything all right? Do you have someone from whom to get the assignment?'" said Alfa Anderson. But creating real relationships takes attentiveness and commitment on the part of teachers, as Josh Thomases explained.

Relationships are created by spending time with young people outside of class, after school, during lunch, checking in with them, saying hello to them in the morning as much as possible, having individual conversations as quickly as possible with all of them . . . trying to know something about them and trying to figure out what is going to be the connection.

Relationships between teachers and students are mutual endeavors. Teachers' behaviors both influence and are influenced by student engagement. Teachers' perceptions of their students' engagement and emotions in elementary school classrooms have been found to predict their subsequent interactions with students across the school year.[20] Not surprisingly, teachers respond most negatively to passive students who are withdrawn from learning activities, and treat children who are already actively engaged in class in a way that encourages them to increase their participation. A model of caring teacher behavior thus requires attention to these patterns of interaction and strategies to overcome natural reactions of neglect or coercion.

Fostering Autonomy in the Classroom

Models of caring teacher-student relationships are not, however, based merely on warmth or affection. Research on the critical mechanisms of the teacher-student relationship stress teacher practices that fulfill basic needs for competence and autonomy. Enhancing feelings of respect and support for personal autonomy are as important as emotional safety and security. Surveys of high school students have found that teacher practices of involving students in decision making are as important or more important as warm and frequent interpersonal interaction as a demonstration of caring.[21] Middle school students asked to articulate characteristics of caring teachers most frequently referred to teaching practices that involved help with schoolwork and that showed respect, value for individuality, and tolerance.[22]

Some of the best strategies for empowering students in the classroom involve deploying democratic, nonauthoritative pedagogical styles that emphasize negotiation and student input.[23] These practices allow students a meaningful voice in both what they will learn and how they will go about learning it. Students also help to determine how their work will be assessed and by what standards quality will be judged. Opening up such fundamentals as curriculum and teaching methods to student input models the kind of challenging, critical thinking that teachers aim to foster. Offering to share ownership of important decisions allows students opportunities for personal investment and real engagement in the classroom. Importantly, when limits and standards must be imposed, teachers do this honestly and explicitly, explaining their actions in terms of the expectations of external authorities and their own responsibilities.

At El Puente, Josh Thomases begins his 11th-grade U.S. history course with brainstorming exercises in which students develop lists of world problems, their causes, and historical reasons. When it becomes obvious that they do not have the answers, students are encouraged to develop lists of questions. This list, supplemented by Thomases' own questions, forms the basis of the curriculum. The class also determines, as a group, what homework will look like, how class time will be spent (in lectures, group work, or discussion), and what measures will be used to assess performance.

Democratic pedagogy also has implications for disciplinary practices. It stresses developing a communal understanding of the norms of behavior and the reasons why such norms are necessary. Misbehavior is seen as a violation against the group, not the teacher's rules. Adherence to behavior expectations is a choice students make in order to participate in the community of the classroom. Facilitators at El Puente often find that freshmen, who are new to the school, need continual retraining to understand this kind of discipline. Individual classrooms reinforce the behavior expectations discussed in freshmen orientation; but real understanding requires frequent, supportive reminders, as Hector Calderòn explained,

> I seldom get into confrontations . . . a lot of the time, what I will say is, "You know our rules, you know how we live here, you have your options. It's up to you what you want to do, but if you can't abide by these things, then you can't be in this community today." I'm not so much getting angry at him, but reminding him, "This is how you agreed to live."

Developing a Curriculum Aimed at Students' Human Potential

Given the importance of respect, autonomy, and tolerance to young people's experience of school, the content of teaching contains as much potential for caring as the context. A "caring curriculum" is one that is oriented toward fostering students' abilities to think critically and developing their capacities to act effectively in their world. At El Puente, the curriculum is organized around teaching students to understand themselves, their community, and their place in the world. "We are trying to teach them that they are sociopolitical beings," explained Hector Calderòn. "Classes should not be something that's simply imposed on [them] . . . but [something that] really allows them to investigate who they are." In the 9th and 10th grades, coursework is organized, as much as possible, around the questions, "Who am I?" and "Who are we?" Junior year is devoted to examining "What do we see around us?" and by their senior year, students are encouraged to ask, "What do we want to do about it?" Last year the seniors in Josh Thomases' Economics class spent a semester undertaking an in-depth study of redlining, the practice of geographically based discrimination by banks. After months studying the political and historical antecedents of the practice, collecting data and performing mathematical analyses, the group presented their findings and recommendations to the Park Bay Area Community Development Team, a local community-based organization. Each student also wrote an individual paper.

The aim of the El Puente curriculum is to teach young people that they have a voice, and that knowledge, combined with their voice, can be real power. Students have frequent opportunities for public speaking, both at school functions and at events in the community. The power of words—in public speech, in letters to political prisoners, and in negotiations within and outside the classroom—is constantly emphasized. As one student explained,

> There are so many options here . . . if you don't like public speaking, you might be able to write something . . . you might express yourself through video . . . This school really tries to teach you don't be silent, don't be quiet, don't just accept everything; you have a say in what goes on. You have a say in what goes on.

Reflecting the Values of the Classroom in the Culture of the School

Although the classroom is the most immediate social context for learning, research on schoolwide environments has shown that the culture and explicit goals of the entire school can contribute to motivation and enhance students' sense of belonging. Large-scale studies of student achievement in high school suggest that the social characteristics of the entire school play an important role in achievement. Schools whose students rated their teachers as more interested in them and committed to teaching reported higher overall academic achievement.[24] Middle school students who describe their school as having less positive relations between teachers and students and being more focused on comparative performance also report lower feelings of academic self-efficacy and lower feelings of belonging and self-worth.[25]

El Puente can achieve this climate of support and belonging in part because it is a small school with staff uniformly committed to the necessity of personal relationships for successful teaching, but equally importantly, because values of caring undergird the mission and operating philosophy of the entire school. From student input in the curriculum to the staff collectives that are charged with developing school policy on several different fronts, El Puente's culture is characterized by discussion, group reflection, and a commitment to community. The values that shape the classroom—relationships with teachers, encouraging students to find their voices, and offering them a meaningful role in classroom decision making—are reflected in schoolwide cultural and administrative practices that encourage relationships between teachers, team teaching and mentoring, and policy input even from the most junior staff.

It is striking that schools that succeed in creating caring climates are generally those that understand the necessity of continually expressing and reaffirming their commitment to a caring atmosphere. They do not take their culture for granted; rather, they often describe themselves as struggling to get it right. The following chapter will examine the strategies of caring schools and other organizations in greater depth.

SPECIAL RELATIONSHIPS: THE IMPACT OF MENTORING

Mentor relationships comprise a special category of caring relationships, distinguished by their intensity, their developmental focus, and their impact on a young person's development into adulthood. Mentoring can be thought of as a natural process of development, allowing an adolescent the opportunity to begin to establish an identity separate from his or her family under the guidance and protection of another parent-like figure. Mentors serve as important sources of social support, offering both instrumental assistance—such as job contacts, introductions to broadening opportunities or situations, and exposure to resources useful in education or career—and personal support and guidance. Mentor relationships are a common and age-old component of the widening circle of individuals who play a part in a person's development, beginning with parents and primary caregivers and extending, during adolescence and early adulthood, to extended family members, neighbors, teachers, work supervisors, and other caring adults.[26]

Although many dramatic stories of mentoring describe the experiences of at-risk youth from dysfunctional families, mentoring is not usually or even ideally a replacement for parenting. Mentor relationships play a natural, complementary role with respect to primary attachment relationships, offering guidance and instruction of a different kind and often on different topics than the parents, and serving as an unbiased supporter of the adolescent's developing autonomy. Some research has suggested, in fact, that adolescents with strong parental relationships may be more capable of and receptive to maintaining supportive mentoring relationships.[27] However, as the Kauai Longitudinal Study and other research has shown, young people at risk for poor social outcomes who have the ability and/or good fortune to engage in mentor relationships gain important positive influences that can protect them from many of the stressors of their existence.

Mentor relationships can be naturally occurring, as often happens in tight-knit communities, or programmatically supported. The role of mentoring in the business world and in specialized scientific fields has been extensively explored.[28] However, mentoring takes place in all sorts of interpersonal contacts and with far less specific goals. "Natural" mentor relationships can be as straightforward as a woman in a community who reaches out to a younger, newly arrived mother, introducing her to other members of the community, helping her get settled, and offering advice on childrearing. An adult in a youth-serving profession may befriend a young man, assist him in negotiating the efforts required to apply to a specialized technical program, and thus help him to become established in an career unrelated to his own.

Natural mentor relationships have been studied primarily in light of their protective qualities in the lives of at-risk youth. Natural mentors have been shown to be an important protective influence in the lives of young, low-income African American and Latina mothers. Young women who were able to identify a natural mentor—usually an older woman from their community—were found to be less depressed, more satisfied with their social resources, and more able to draw needed benefits from their social networks.[29] Pregnant teens with natural mentor relationships are less likely to drop out of school and more likely to hold a job in the years following childbirth than are pregnant teens without mentors.[30]

The last ten years have seen major growth in programmatically supported relationships, those operating with the support of such mentoring organizations as Big Brothers/Big Sisters and One to One, or arising from school- or community-based intervention programs. Although some of these programs work to connect inner-city youths with adults of different socioeconomic backgrounds, many are designed to employ community members, teachers, and other adults in more intensive roles with the young people around them. Mentoring programs have also become popular approaches to helping at-risk youths succeed in middle and high school. However, the quality and intensity of mentoring programs in schools is highly variable.[31]

Among some policy makers and youth service professionals, mentoring has lost credibility as a means of supporting and guiding youth development in light of studies that have shown limited or no impact of mentoring relationships. Unfortunately, many of these research findings report on mentor relationships of varying duration; and research has shown that relationships might need to exist for a year or more before any significant effects can be found.[32] Research also suggests that in many cases the failure of mentoring as a strategy for serving young people has been a result of the failure of the sponsoring program to support, guide, and encourage intensive, sustainable mentoring relationships. The wide divergence in results of evaluations of mentoring programs underscores the importance of developing and maintaining positive relationship practices—including demanding a long-term commitment from mentors—among programmatically supported mentoring relationships.

A review of the literature suggests several important components of positive and effective mentor relationships. First, contact between the mentor and the young person needs to be frequent and regular enough that a real relationship can develop and the young person can develop trust and confidence in the mentor's availability to him. Successful mentor relationships involve a major commitment of time and attention on the part of the mentor.[33] Second, mentor relationships in which youths are viewed as individuals to be supported rather than problems to be solved appear to have a greater likelihood of succeeding as positive, influential, and sustainable relationships.[34] A study of mentor relationships initiated by Big Brothers/Big Sisters programs found that most positive mentor relationships, like most healthy relationships of any kind, were characterized by time, trust, respect, and compromise. Successful volunteer mentors took time to establish and maintain their charge's trust; they listened rather than lectured when youths raised disturbing issues; they respected a youth's interests and desires and encouraged joint decision making and compromise in the terms of the relationship, shared activities, and communication.[35]

MEASURING CARE: VALUING THE PROCESS

The sections above summarizing the research evidence of the role of caring in development have avoided questions of how caring is measured or even identified. However, it is not clear that caring has yet been defined as a measurable property that can be assessed by standard methods. Although there is some consensus on what caring looks like as an input to development or a desired outcome, researchers are not always measuring the same things. Methods for evaluating care and its impact range from interviews to questionnaires, and from quantitative results such as grades or measurable behaviors to qualitative, ethnographic evidence.

Studies focused on the impact of care on development have used diverse methods to measure the care a young person receives from parents, teachers, friends, and others. Most prominent among these are questionnaires that measure an individual's perception of how others feel about him or her and of the availability and willingness of others to offer help and support. Many of these questionnaires assess the caring and support provided by parents and within the family; others measure social support available throughout a young person's social sphere.[36] A number of researchers have developed measures of young people's perceptions of their social contexts in order to gain a means of distinguishing environments that facilitate healthy development.[37] There are inherent problems with "self-report" measures, as these kinds of questionnaires are called. Subjects might not be honest about their feelings and might bias their answers to socially desirable responses or toward what they think the researcher wants to hear. Moreover, their perceptions might not accurately reflect their relationships with others. However, it is quite possible that in the realm of caring, support, and acceptance, perception is more important than reality: if caring works to create a sense of security and acceptance in which positive development can occur, then its perceived presence is, arguably, the only reality that matters.

Measuring caring is difficult when circumstances, culture, and individual differences produce different caring behaviors. Caring looks different in different contexts, and caring behavior varies across culture and circumstance. Any attempt to identify caring must be flexible enough to accommodate different practices of care among different groups and in a variety of circumstances.

Similar questions arise when one attempts to evaluate the development of caring qualities in young people. Caring encompasses competencies, attitudes, and behaviors, each of which must be measured in its own way. Some of the best studies of caring in adolescents employ multiple methods and elicit information from peers and adults as well as the adolescent in question.[38] Other researchers have included measures of caring behavior in assessing caring individuals. In a longitudinal study of how individual, family, and environmental factors in early childhood are related to the development of caring in adolescence, researchers are assessing caring through measures of volunteering, self-rating scales, and prosocial moral reasoning.[39] Unfortunately, preliminary results suggest little correlation between volunteering activities and measures of caring attitudes and competence.[40]

Finally, a few researchers have begun to examine caring attitudes, or empathy, through studies of affective reactions to situations in which caring is needed. Subjects are videotaped as they watch scenarios designed to elicit caring responses, and their nonverbal behavior is studied for evidence of empathic concern for the people in need of help.[41]

By far the most common method of assessing caring attitudes is through questionnaires in which young people are asked how strongly they agree or disagree with or how well they are described by statements that assess dimensions of empathy and concern for others.[42] Studies of the impact of youth community service have often employed measures of individual and social responsibility, most notably the Social and Personal Responsibility Scale, a questionnaire that explores young people's attitudes about social welfare and duty, and their feelings of competence and efficacy.[43] These self-rating scales, as discussed above, tend to elicit responses biased toward socially acceptable answers and towards self-enhancement. However, many have been shown to produce reliable differences across individuals.

Many of the reasons why care is hard to measure arise from the qualities of care itself. Care is individually focused, so that each person's experience is unique. There is no "standard treatment," in research parlance, that can be evaluated across groups. The effects of caring in organized care situations depend as much on the individual's starting point and contribution to the relationship as on the efforts of a caregiver. Individuality and mutuality are essential values of care, but also part of the reason care is so difficult to measure.

Organized opportunities for care of adolescents, in particular, are also distinguished by diversity, fluidity, and a wide range of options with respect to structure, organization, and activities. As young people make the transition from childhood to adolescence, they are more and more involved in choosing their activities and how they spend their time. Individual preferences and self-selection begin to determine activities, much more so than for younger children. One youth might be drawn to extracurricular sports, while another might find a less structured activity away from school. Some young people will look for more intense, personal relationships with adults in organized care situations, while others will prefer more instrumental relationships. One size does not fit all in organized care experiences, so having diversity of experiences and opportunities to choose from is essential. But again, this diversity causes problems when seeking to measure care's effects.

The limitations inherent in measuring caring and its effects raise the essential question of how we as a society decide how to invest in efforts that, despite our conviction of their value, do not demonstrate significant measurable benefits in quantitative research. The existing body of research on caring suggests that the experience of being cared for and caring for others might be too variable between individuals to measure their effects in a standardized format. Moreover, it might be impossible to isolate and quantify the impact of any individual aspect of a normal developmental process. The absence of a means to identify and measure the effect of a variable does not imply that it is of no value; however, our social and public policy efforts are driven by outcomes and dominated by cost-benefit analyses. We tend to value that which we can measure. An important challenge facing researchers studying caring and its effects on development is to articulate a set of reasonable expectations for the extent to which caring can have an impact and the extent to which this impact can be quantified.

Even if one could surmount the difficulties of measuring caring, a focus on specific outcomes might miss the most important effect of caring: the creation of social connectedness and the orientation towards engagement with others. The time and attention that both adults and young people in organized care settings devote to care relationships might have the primary effect of binding young people to social connections that promote stability and interdependence. Organized care settings are often vital centers of belonging in a young person's life. Relational psychologists maintain that social connection is essential to healthy development and social functioning; social and political thinkers argue that social connections through informal institutions are of value in and of themselves.[44]

Social connectedness might well be the primary effect of caring. The indicators of healthy social functioning described in previous sections might be secondary effects, arising from these basic developments. Certainly, research on school climates has demonstrated that academic achievement, low absenteeism, and other positive behaviors are likely consequences of school connectedness. Given the importance of social connectedness, evaluations of caring practices ought to be less concerned with outcome-driven measures and more focused on the ways in which these social connections form.

If forming connections is what is important in caring, then we should look at the process of caring itself to evaluate care. Focusing on the process of caring means observing the behaviors and interactions that comprise a caring relationship, as opposed to presumed changes in the one cared for. It means gauging the quality of care with reference to the model of attentiveness, responsiveness, and competence presented in earlier chapters. It means saying that a program has accomplished its goals if it has succeeded in creating caring relationships between young people and positive role models.

Focusing on the process of care is also more consistent with the spirit of caring itself. Care is a process, not a means to an end: attentive care is directed to the one cared for, not external goals. Caring has value in and of itself, as well as for the outcomes it produces.

This, of course, is how most of us approach caring in parenting and other aspects of daily life. We invest ourselves in our children not only because we believe that doing so will lead to positive outcomes; we do so primarily because we value the process of care itself. We have some implicit belief that caring is important that is based not on research of its effects but on a common-sense, heartfelt belief in its value.

The leap of faith required in this argument is to believe that intentional care can have similar effects as the spontaneous, naturally occurring care that occurs in families and other settings. The research in this chapter offers some preliminary evidence that organized, intentional care can have meaningful impact. More research in this area is clearly needed to explain how and under what circumstances organized care settings can impact development. However, the nature of caring is such that we will never have the quantitative documentation of caring's effects that an outcome-driven perspective requires. Development is too complex and individualized, and caring too qualitative, to be captured in numerical measures.

But a qualitative approach does not have to be, in Frances Lucerna's words, "merely touchy-feely." The quality of the caring process can be a rigorous indicator. We can look critically and specifically at the process of caring to distinguish positive behaviors and practices from unconstructive ones, competent responses from inappropriate ones, and attentive, individually focused efforts from less thoughtful ones. We can look at what practices are meant to convey to young people, and how they are interpreted by them. We can gauge whether caregivers in organized care settings are truly responsive to young people, or whether their responses are bureaucratic or formulaic. In other words, we can examine the quality of the caregiving process and from that examination conclude that the experience is of value to the young people participating.

CHAPTER 6

SUSTAINING CARE: CARING SCHOOLS AND OTHER ORGANIZATIONS

The drive up County Road 25 to Smokey House Center in Danby, Vermont, is spectacular, but nothing quite prepares you for the view upon entering the driveway. Nestled in pristine verdant mountains, overlooking cornfields and rolling green pastures where cows and horses silently graze, a classic Vermont farmhouse sits on a broad lawn. Weathered outbuildings and a stone shed that is a work of art in itself complete the picture. The grounds are impeccably maintained: country flowers spill out of window boxes, large trees shelter picnic tables, a thick carpet of grass leads out to fields in the distance. Smokey House looks like a tourist's dream, but it is in fact a working farm created for and maintained by adolescents who learn teamwork, responsibility, and respect in a year-round experiential learning program. The physical grounds the young people work so hard to keep up reflect the culture and values of the program itself. "It's peaceful here," explained Sean, an 11th-grader who's been working at Smokey House for three years. "Nobody shouts; nobody yells at you."

Smokey House Center is a thoughtfully constructed work environment for 14- to 17-year-old students whose schools have identified them as at risk for failure in or disruptive to the school environment. Young people apply to the program through a formal application and review process. During the school year, approximately 25 students commute as many as 30 miles to work every afternoon, tending crops, caring for farm animals, husbanding the center's several thousand acres of forest land, and producing charcoal, firewood, maple syrup, and Christmas trees for sale in nearby communities. In the summer, the Center offers 40 or more students full-time employment for eight weeks. The young people work in teams of six, trained and supervised by adult crew leaders who offer exposure to the standards of the workplace along with support and guidance.

Smokey House's staff have worked hard to create an environment at the Center in which young people can feel a part of a community that values them. Building community is a multifaceted effort, arising from standards of how staff relate to each other and to the young people who work with them, from shared expectations about work and behavior, and from traditions that lend Smokey House a sense of stability and dependability. At Smokey House, such traditions include ongoing volleyball tournaments and weekly circle meetings attended by all staff. They are also embedded in relationships and in actions. "Many things that you might not think of in that way can be considered tradition," explained Tim Parent, Crew Coordinator at Smokey House. "A joke between a crew leader and a crew member, for example, may be a tradition, maybe a brief one that happens over a few months." Tim described a young man who came to Smokey House with a fantastic story about seeing a brown pelican in Rutland that turned into an ongoing joke between the two of them for over two years. "It was something that we shared in common and could always depend on to laugh about . . . whenever it was brought up, it was going to be something that we both valued."

Actions that young people can count on, day in and day out, are also important in community building. Tim makes a point of greeting the bus that brings students to Smokey House every day "so that they [the students] can know I'm always going to be here standing here waiting for the bus when it shows up . . . that's a tradition, too."

Smokey House is an example of how caring can bridge the territory between interpersonal relationships and an organization. At Smokey House, the caring attitudes and behaviors of individuals are institutionalized in the Center's values, procedures, and even in its physical space. The Center's appearance, and the role the young people have in maintaining it, is an important part of Smokey House's effort to create a caring environment. The beauty and organization of the farm is a product of the young workers' efforts, and that fact is its most important value. Their care for this beautiful place gives the young people at Smokey House both pride in their surroundings and a sense of belonging to them. Just as the Whitings found in their cross-cultural research, contributing to one's environment both builds competence and helps one feel engaged in a mutual process.

But place is not just about scenery and facilities. It is, most important, about an environment where young people are encouraged to behave in ways that show self-respect and respect for others. Toward these ends, Smokey House has institutionalized practices that facilitate caring relationships and demonstrate strategies for respectful interaction.

Lynn Bondurant, Smokey House's executive director, feels that establishing clear expectations and understood consequences of behavior are key to creating a safe and caring environment. Each crew at Smokey House begins a summer or school program with meetings to discuss what they expect of each other and of the crew leader, and what the crew leader can expect of them, along with a discussion of the consequences of not meeting those expectations. "When new students come in at the beginning of the year, we sit down and talk about expectations and rules. We also talk about respect. A lot of these kids don't really know what respect means." Hope Requardt, a crew leader, explained.

> We have the kids write down their expectations, and one of the first questions is, "How do you expect to be treated?" . . . I had three kids in my crew who said, "I don't mind if you call me names, and I don't mind if you hit me." And I said, "I am not going to have you guys have that as an expectation." . . . a lot of the time they need to have safe limits set for them in terms of behavior.

Weekly circle meetings, at which crews report on activities and request help from other groups, problems are discussed, and plans made, are important venues for modeling respectful interaction. The Center has a rule that in order to speak, one must be holding the "talking sack," a plain burlap bag. Everyone waits his turn and has to be given leave to speak by the others in the group. Daily crew meetings and frequent one-on-one contact with crew leaders and the crew coordinator establish a climate in which problems are surfaced and worked through collectively. "One crew might have a problem with name-calling, or a boy and a girl who are too touchy-feely, or something like that," explained Lynn. "So the crew will sit down and talk about how it is disrespectful, and that we want to treat each other how we want to be treated . . . It is a slow process, but as problems emerge the crew leaders try to work through them."

The staff has also learned to treat discipline as an opportunity to model alternatives to authoritarian behavior and adversarial relationships. "When I first came here eight years ago it was much more authoritarian, a little like boot camp," said Tim Parent. "I can remember raising my voice a lot and not having it work well." Crew leaders are now encouraged to help their charges select choices rather than prescribing courses of action for them. Previously, the basic form of discipline was docking, sitting out without pay. "When I became crew coordinator, the more I saw docking on a crew, the less effective I thought that crew leader was being," said Tim. Smokey House now has an explicit disciplinary procedure in which positive reminders and reinforcements, along with modeling and prompting, are the first lines of discipline. If a crew has a problem—a crew member who fails to do his share of the work, for instance—the crew is expected to discuss the problem internally first; if no progress is made, a circle meeting of all crews may be called. Tim has also formalized a distinction between docking, which is punitive, and timeout, which does not involve going off the clock. "Timeout says that it is important enough to us that you resolve a problem that we are giving you paid time to do it," he explained.

As a last resort, a crew leader will recommend that a young person be removed from the crew. To be reinstated, a young person must come up with a plan, in the form of a contract between himself, the crew leader, and Tim, the crew coordinator. The contract defines a problem, suggests solutions, and describes the consequences of failing to perform the agreed-upon solutions. Smokey House is committed to ensuring that young people meet the consequences of their actions, and attempts to enforce them consistently. "You confuse a kid when you say that something is going to be a consequence of their choices and actions, and then the consequences don't come," said Lynn Bondurant. "I think, too, that you are telling them that you didn't really believe they could do what was asked of them."

Smokey House staff believe caring for youth demands that one consistently hold them to high expectations. There are many rules at Smokey House—crew members must wear uniforms and behave professionally on the job, participation at the Center is predicated on attending school and keeping up with schoolwork, and behavior that is unsafe or unfair to others is prohibited—but to the greatest extent possible, the rules are set up as expectations that the young person must choose to meet. Smokey House sees part of its role as teaching young people the skills to understand and meet the expectations of a group, specifically a workplace. "If you pull the standards back for those young people who are not able to meet those expectations, that is not caring," explained Lynn Bondurant. "They will never be able to make the choice to participate if they don't develop the skills."

Developing these skills requires constant coaching, as well as articulated standards. "In school I think they are basically told to sit still and behave, and I don't think that they are listened to, or given constructive methods to deal with their problems," said Hope Requardt. "But here if they are not behaving right, we tell them that is not the right way, but then we give them suggestions about what the right way might be, so they have an out." In addition to the goal setting and planning that takes place up front, young people are evaluated by their crew leaders according to benchmarks at key points during their experience. The benchmarks cover behavior, reliability, and the quality of their work. A system that has well-established mechanisms for discussing problems, such as crew meetings and circle meetings, allows young people to experience constructive problem solving and talking out differences firsthand.

Similarly, when a young person fails to meet the expectations of the job, he or she is rarely out-and-out fired. "Nobody leaves without an open-door policy," says Lynn Bondurant. Termination discussions focus on what the young person can do to become a successful applicant in the future. "If they are allowed to reapply, almost always, those kids are successful, because they lost something due to their actions and they know," said Lynn Bondurant. "They have to have that learning experience in order to get there."

The careful attention to individual development, the climate of choice rather than prescriptions, and the institutionalized standards of respect are ways in which Smokey House has intentionally created a caring organization. For some young people in difficult home circumstances and not succeeding in school, exposure to the ways in which people relate to each other at Smokey House can be a transforming experience. "I'm much more relaxed than I used to be," explained Sean, reflecting on his three years at Smokey House. "Here, the way people talk to each other, it just makes you not worry so much."

"I used to have a really mean attitude toward everyone," said Donna, after her first summer at Smokey House. "I feel like I have changed from watching other people, and how they are acting."

Smokey House is a refuge, but it is very careful to balance the goal of buffering its charges from some of the more discouraging aspects of their lives with preparing them to deal successfully with the realities of adult expectations. Although its careful attention to developing responsibility and promoting positive choices is clearly valuable, its most important lesson for the young people who work there might be that respectful, positive relationships can be an option for them in the future. If there is one important message that the adults at Smokey House are trying to convey, it is that places like Smokey House are worth striving for, worth getting an education for, and worth trying to create elsewhere in their lives. "One of the things that we try to work on with kids," said Lynn Bondurant, "is that if they are in a place where they are respected and they feel good that they can make choices to look for those kinds of places—in work, school and experiences—in the future, that it's something they can ask for."

*   *   *

Caring for youth is rarely an individual experience. More often, out-of-family care for young people occurs in the context of a program, organization, or other intentional setting in which the place, as well as the people who work there, becomes important to the young person. Creating a sense of place to which young people can attach requires an organized structure of some kind, something greater than the sum of individual relationships. This structure can exert powerful influences in the lives of young people. The opportunities and resources a school or other institution can offer can be effective attractions to engage a youth, and its culture can foster compelling group norms.

Schools and other youth-serving organizations can be more or less intentionally structured and can be more or less oriented toward care as their organizing principle. Regardless of intentionality, all organizations transmit messages to the youths they serve. Norms of interaction among and between youths and staff, the ways that decisions are made, groups are structured, time is allocated and many other practices contain implicit values. Organizations that demonstrate fairness and consistency while valuing the needs of the individual are modeling competent care to the young people who encounter them. Organizations that intentionally concern themselves with the entirety of a young person's life teach the value of attentiveness.

Similarly, an organization can more or less effectively facilitate care in the extent to which it offers support and guidance to adults who invest themselves personally in young people. An organization that cares for its caregivers helps replenish its most important resource, the emotional energy of those whose time is spent in direct contact with youth. This resource is in constant demand. Building a climate of trust and safety in which a young person can feel comfortable discussing problems often involves investing a great deal of time. It also requires a commitment to share oneself, to open up to a young person and reveal the fragility, confusion, and uniqueness that are present in all of us, but which young people sometimes feel is theirs alone. "Part of the reason I feel like I can let my normal self out here," said Leslie, a fifteen-year-old at Smokey House, "is that the crew leaders are letting their normal selves out too."

This chapter will explore how the practices, structure, and philosophies of schools and other organizations can model caring values and facilitate care by the individuals who work for them and the youths they serve. Relationships with caring adults draw much of their power from the voluntary nature of the experience; they are cooperative, not coercive experiences for a young person. Young people must take on some responsibility for the care relationship, and it is in this process that constructive engagement can occur. An institution can foster these relationships by adopting specific practices that demonstrate attentiveness, responsiveness, and competence, the hallmarks of caring organizations as well as caring individuals. These practices are a natural and consistent outgrowth of intentionally applying the tenets of care to organizational structure, philosophy, and mission.

PROVIDING CARE BEYOND THE FAMILY

Care provided in organized settings has unique characteristics. By their nature voluntary associations, relationships between young people and caregivers outside of the family are predicated on both parties "being here willingly," as Tim Parent described it. Many organized care providers, including experiential learning centers like Smokey House, are optional associations for adolescents. While education is compulsory for most of adolescence, connection to the purpose and values of school—and the commitment to continue and succeed at education—is similarly voluntary. A young person passes judgment on an organized care provider simply by choosing to attend; or if forced to attend, by choosing to engage. Thus a major emphasis for those that seek to educate and care for youth is on creating a context that is inviting and attractive to young people.

Such a context usually involves specific activities or events in which young people participate. In some cases, such as The Warming House or the Block Brothers program, activities are primarily structured or unstructured fun experiences that draw a young person in to form more significant relationships with program staff. In other cases, such as the National Indian Youth Leadership Project or Smokey House Center, the activities are meant to offer opportunities to experience accomplishment, teamwork, and responsibility. At El Puente, a range of extracurricular activities is designed to foster relationships with teachers and other adults outside the classroom. Some organizations have designed activities—such as caring for children, the elderly, or animals—whose content helps young people practice targeted values. As Lynn Bondurant of Smokey House explained:

> For many of these kids it is easier to make the connections between caring and their behavior when the object of their care is an animal, or plants . . . We had one young man here who had a terrible time getting along with the other kids but was absolutely devoted to our old horse . . . and it was through his caring for that horse that he relaxed and became able to understand what it meant to care for another person.

Regardless of the activity, organized care providers invariably attract youth by creating a sense of a group which, like a family, offers opportunities for belonging. These settings can be venues for young people to experience acceptance and valuing of themselves as individuals, experiences that might not be available to them in school or even at home. Importantly, such settings generally avoid judgments that can alienate or exclude potential participants.

At the same time, one of the great attractions of these organizations is that they are not families. They offer opportunities for a young person to break free of the parent-child relationship and begin to learn mature, responsible life habits on an independent basis, while protected and guided by caring adults. Nonfamily "families" can also be opportunities for young people to try on new identities in their struggle to create an adult self. The relationships built between young people and adults in these organizations, and between young people and each other, can be more egalitarian and more mutual than might be possible at home. Unrelated adults and other role models can model behavior and demonstrate strategies for caring and coping that might be more difficult to absorb if coming from parents.

The opportunities available in nonfamily organized care relationships are balanced by corresponding challenges. Teachers and other unrelated adults do not have the benefit of ingrained trust; it is usually built gradually rather than granted automatically. In schools and other youth-serving organizations, trust is not simply a matter between two individuals. A young person must come to trust the organization as well, to believe that the organization itself is safe, reliable, and fair. Likewise, it is not enough for a young person to know and be understood by a single individual; she must feel as well that she knows and is connected to the organization as well.

The best caring organizations, such as Smokey House Center, offer young people firsthand exposure to what a caring place ought to look like. However, many young people do not know what they are looking for, and this creates challenges as well. An excellent program might not be a good match with an individual's needs and temperament. A young person searching for care might put her trust in an unsupervised, ill-trained adult. Troubled youths with few social supports are particularly vulnerable to irresponsible caregivers who lack the capability or intention to offer age-appropriate, well supervised care. While adolescents are old enough to decide which places and activities they prefer, they need guidance in choosing programs and support in developing judgment about relationships.

The voluntary nature of most organized care settings creates powerful contexts for growth and development. Not surprisingly, trust and engagement are easier to build in a voluntary, as opposed to coercive, environment.[1] It is in choosing to belong that a young person begins to open himself to be influenced. "Being here willingly" is the first step to adopting the values of the organization. Young people are open and responsive to guidance because they want to be a part of the school or program in question. They are willing to follow rules if that is what it takes to participate.

The special characteristics of organized care requires that its guidance take the form of indirect influence rather than prescriptions or judgments. Although personal judgments are often counterproductive, group norms and standards are very effective means of exposing young people to caring behaviors and values. Some of these norms may be explicit: NIYLP prohibits t-shirts that celebrate alcoholic products: at Smokey House circle meetings, anyone who wishes to speak must wait until the "talking sack" is passed to him. Many important messages, however, are often subtly and implicitly conveyed. Smoking among adolescents is a concern for many youth workers; as one explained, "It's hard to be caring and ignore things that are destructive." Yet lectures do little to address the problem; all teenagers know that smoking is bad for them. Instead, as Tim Parent of Smokey House explained, "We're not going to dictate, but we try to offer messages that suggest options." At Smokey House, smoking is only permitted in a specific area set apart from the group, and only during break times. The breaks are devoted to team volleyball and basketball tournaments, so young people must choose between smoking and participating in group games. Hiking and camping trips are set to the pace of nonsmokers, leaving smokers huffing and puffing. More than one participant at Smokey House has quit smoking for the incentive of racing Tim up a mountain.

The strongest messages about caring come from the ways that caring values are institutionalized and consistently applied throughout an organization. Thoughtful, consistent behavior on the part of individual staffers can create group norms about mutual respect, trust, and acceptance. But an organization can reinforce messages about caring by instituting practices that reward these norms and demonstrate that they are effective strategies of interaction. Young people are more likely to internalize caring values if they see that such values are important enough to shape the practices of the adult world they observe.

WHAT IS A CARING ORGANIZATION?

The best way to teach care is by modeling it in every phase of an organization. Caring organizations are characterized by ongoing attention to consistency between the messages they preach to young people and the messages encoded in their actions. They are, for the most part, highly intentional places.

First and foremost, caring organizations are characterized by respect for and protection of the youths they serve. They work to develop experienced staff who clearly understand the developmental needs of young people. They structure accountability, oversight, and training into their operations to protect staff and youths alike. They support, rather than compete with, a young person's family and culture.

The most salient characteristic of caring organizations is a spirit, or atmosphere, of respect and trust. Staff of organizations that think carefully about caring often respond that this atmosphere is the most important aspect of their organization and the one that they work at hardest. Caring atmospheres are to some extent self-perpetuating, in that once they exist, new members of the organization both anticipate the climate and learn from veterans how to perform in it. But they are also tenuous, in that they require consistent attention and ongoing time and effort to maintain. "Modeling care at every stage of the organization forces us to hold ourselves to very high standards," explained Lynn Bondurant of Smokey House. "It means we have to act thoughtfully and consistently at every step, even when it might be easier in the short run to manage some things another way."

One of the most important ways that caring organizations sustain their special spirit is by caring for all participants, not just the youths they serve. Caring organizations work to create a culture in which staff and often parents feel as though "they don't have to do it alone," as one director put it. They are places that understand the value of interpersonal relationships and are willing to devote the organizational time and energy toward maintaining them. They are places, for example, that see mentoring as appropriate for adult relationships as well as for relationships between adults and youths. They are places that recognize the entirety of their staffs' lives just as they work to recognize this for youths and are willing to devote institutional resources to support their staffs' personal growth, balance of work and family life, and empowerment.

In an earlier chapter care was described as an interactive process involving attentiveness, responsiveness, and competence. Attentiveness can be thought of as the inclination and capacity to consider each individual as unique, having a set of needs, desires, and circumstances that are hers alone. Responsiveness, the motivation to care, can be considered the will to engage in quality caregiving for young people. Competence involves the ability to meet an individual's needs, including having the knowledge and experience to care effectively and the capability to provide what is needed.

In an organizational context, these terms have different practical connotations, but their basic meanings are the same. An organization that values attentiveness will work hard at training staff to demonstrate that they are listening to the young people they serve. It will also formally concern itself with the entirety of a young person's life, requiring that youth workers know what is going on for a young person at home, at school, and in other contexts. It will concern itself, for example, with transportation, safety, and other issues not directly related to program activities but essential to the young person's experience.

Responsiveness in organized care settings refers directly to organizational philosophy and mission. What are the terms on which the organization accepts its mission to serve its target population? The individual youths who participate? Responsiveness bespeaks commitment to a quality of relationship between the program and each young person involved (while recognizing that not every young person will succeed to the organization's expectations), quality that requires meaningful investment in understanding and building relationships with each participant.

Competence in organizations relates to the quality of the product—caring relationships—that the organization provides. Competent organizations are those that have structured themselves to ensure that caregivers are properly trained, experienced and supervised; and that the organization has the resources and capacity to accept responsibility for the youths in their care.

In addition to the intentionally structured programs profiled in this book, initiatives that have experimented with ways of redirecting the social atmosphere and values of organizations can be understood in terms of this model. One of the most famous of these initiatives is the Comer Schools Movement, a successful school reform project based on the work of James Comer, a child psychiatrist at Yale University.[2] In 1968, Comer and his colleagues began an intervention and research program in two almost exclusively African American and economically disadvantaged elementary schools in New Haven, Connecticut. Surrounded by the alienation, anger, distrust, hopelessness, and despair of the inner city, these schools had the worst achievement, attendance, and behavior records in the city. The Comer Schools Movement is an attempt to improve schools by changing structural and administrative practices to facilitate and develop caring behaviors and attitudes.

The Comer Schools Movement is founded on the assumption that mental health is an essential prerequisite to academic achievement, and that many of the learning and behavior problems students face are rooted in the social stresses of their environment. The Comer model stresses attentiveness to the individual: to his circumstances, the entirety of his experience, and his specific needs. Comer schools have been particularly designed to address the socioemotional challenges of economically disadvantaged groups. As James Comer explained:

> We had to develop an intervention that dealt with dependency, that dealt with the feeling that there was no future and no sense of control. We also

focused on the underdevelopment of the children who came from families that were under severe pressure.[3]

Comer's method of intervention focuses on the organizational management of the school to improve the quality of relationships among teachers, administrators, and parents and to develop a climate of trust in which teaching and learning can take place. An important aspect of Comer's reform work is developing competence: importing mental health knowledge and skills into the school environment, and giving teachers and other adults in the school the skills to understand and support the development of their students. Each school creates a "mental health team" to work with individuals with more severe behavior problems and to help other groups within the school function.

The Comer model also requires a commitment from everyone involved in the child's education, including parents, to work to change their "way of doing business." It demands a new level of responsiveness from teachers, administrators, and parents, all of whom have new responsibilities and shared authority in the new management of the school. And the model is specifically designed to encourage responsiveness as a habit of all interactions with children, rather than solely in reaction to problems.

Ongoing research from another reform effort, the Child Development Project, has shown that reorganizing a school in the service of caring values can influence school climate and student achievement. A demonstration project underway in a dozen elementary schools across the country, the Child Development Project attempts to apply principles of caring both to the classroom and to the structure, practices, and social organization of the school. The Project has sought to create "caring communities of learning" characterized by feelings of mutual concern and respect and by the knowledge that each cares about the welfare and progress of others and that others are responsive and ready to give support when needed. In addition to fostering a climate of care in the classroom, the Project involves enhancing connections between school and family, school and community, and between different classes and teachers within the school. Evaluations of this demonstration project have found that individual students' sense of community, in both demonstration schools and comparison schools, is significantly associated with almost all measures of student outcomes. Some of the strongest positive effects of school community occurred among schools with the most disadvantaged student populations.[4]

These examples illustrate how caring organizations attend, first and foremost, to consistency between their mission and their actions. They recognize that their actions convey messages, and that young people have a sharp eye for inconsistencies between saying and doing. Staff of caring organizations are obsessed with the meanings implicit in their practices, and spend considerable organizational effort on planning and thinking through the content of these practices.

CARING BY DESIGN: ORGANIZATIONAL PRACTICES

Although there are no formulas for creating caring organizations, some specific practices are characteristic of caring schools and high-quality youth programs. These practices reinforce one another and arise from a consistent focus on respect and interdependence. They are designed not only to allow individuals to care for youth more effectively but to create, in the words of Frances Lucerna of El Puente Academy for Peace and Justice, "a community where it is repeated in so many ways that we are responsible to each other—that our actions really have an effect on everybody."

Modeling Caring in Everyday Behavior

Administrators at many caring organizations described a culture, or atmosphere of support as the most important aspect of their organization. This climate arises from norms of interaction that value respect, mutual support, and generosity. Caring organizations actively develop these norms and work to maintain them. At Smokey House, norms include a prohibition against screaming and shouting. "We don't react to each other," explained Lynn Bondurant. "We act together, but we try to anticipate, to understand, but not to react emotionally."

Despite the fact that such norms are shaped at the top of an organization, they are sustained by long-tenured staff who understand caring values and are naturally inclined to caring behaviors. Hiring the right people becomes an important part of creating the right feel for an organized care provider. Lynn Bondurant says she looks for staff "who understand the human condition, who enjoy it and rejoice in it good and bad." Most of the Smokey House job application consists of fictional situations for which the applicant is asked to describe what he or she would do. Lynn looks for applicants "who look for the meaning behind actions, not to excuse or condone them, but to try to change patterns of behavior." A part of this method of reasoning, she believes, is to avoid accusations and value judgments so as to more constructively understand why a young person acts as he does.

Modeling caring in everyday behavior means that every administrative decision is approached from the perspective of its impact on culture and climate. El Puente has refused to install a metal detector at its school, despite the dangers of its neighborhood, and hired a security guard only when it was mandated by the state. "It is not acceptable in this community for us to have a metal detector," explained Frances Lucerna. "Safety needs to come from the individual relationships we build with students . . . it is about trust. And if it is something that is imposed, [as in] 'We will have a metal detector to make you safe,' is that really making you safe?"

Disciplinary practices have a significant impact on organizational culture. Discipline can be punitive or, as described at Smokey House, a constructive learning process. "For both staff and youth, we try to treat honest mistakes as learning lessons," said Lynn Bondurant. "Instead of creating confrontational situations where the door closes," explained Frances Lucerna of El Puente, "I try to offer them some kind of strategy; I give them options, and let them decide." At The Warming House, staff try to use instances of unacceptable behavior as opportunities to help young people understand the consequences of their actions. Adrienne Felder Mittelman explained:

> We make sure that we don't just say, "You can't say that here. Saying that is bad. You need to leave." We make sure that we sit down with them, and say, "Have you thought about this? You know, what do you expect people to think when you talk to them this way or behave this way?"

A caring atmosphere is supported by practices that stress service, communality, and shared purpose. NIYLP staff believe that the presence of many committed adult volunteers at their summer camp contributes to a climate where "people are giving a lot of themselves to the process." At Smokey House, there is an expectation among the crew leaders that no one leaves for the day until everyone's work is done. Nate Smith encourages the Block Brothers to volunteer with him in community-service projects throughout Kansas City. Hector Calderòn explained that new facilitators quickly become "El Puentisized" because "the air that you breathe, everybody's talking [about] this . . . nobody leaves at 3:00. The projects, by their very nature, their intensity, require that you stay after school . . . And then, those people who buy into that, and say, 'this is the way I could live' stay; those that can't, don't."

Articulating Values

Caring organizations are not value-neutral. They hold strong values and communicate them to the young people they serve. Most regard the teaching of values to be one of their most important, and intentional, activities.

Mac Hall of NIYLP believes that inattention to traditionally held values—arising from racism and generations of disrupted families and communities—

has caused much of the frustration and hopeless behavior he sees in Native American youths and their families. "Our whole way of working is designed to balance exposing kids to these values and not making anyone defensive about their own family or community," he explained. Staff both model and explicitly articulate traditional values, such as service, generosity, and cooperation, "but not by lecturing . . . by showing them by example."

When done responsibly, communicating values is rarely a facile exercise. Many times it requires teachers or other youth workers to take unpopular stands that are not completely understood by young people. Part of caring, however, is demonstrating a commitment to hold young people to standards higher that those they might set for themselves. Frances Lucerna, El Puente's principal and a former dance teacher, described her ongoing efforts to help members of the El Puente dance ensemble understand the messages they communicate through their choices of clothes, music, and movements:

> I was always after them, saying, "Think of how you want to represent yourselves, as young women, especially as young women of color— what messages do you want to convey?" . . . Sometimes they'd pick music, and I'd say, "Did you really listen to those lyrics? What do they say?" Or they'd choreograph something, and I'd say, "Let's take another look at that movement . . . It might be ok for a club, but up on a stage, what kind of message does it send?" . . . And gradually they understood that there were certain standards, certain expectations at El Puente . . . But last year we did a study of sweatshops and then some students did a dance about the oppression of women in sweatshops at the Superintendent's Arts Festival. And the girls came back to El Puente, and it was one of those wonderful moments when they get it . . . They reflected on the differences between their dance and other dances, which had provocative moves or suggestive music, and they said, "Now we understand what you've been talking about . . . Now we see it."

Though most schools and many youth organizations are publicly funded, the values of community, respect, and caring in no way overstep the boundaries between church and state. In fact, staff of many caring organizations feel that most schools and other institutions have overreacted to these concerns, eliminating attention to values altogether. "I think society has pigeon-holed practices, so for example, the kind of feeling and spirit that we try to promote every day here at El Puente is the kind of spirit that people expect to feel religiously," said Luis Garden Acosta. "As if public school were a place where values were left at the schoolhouse door . . . a bland, cold, abstract place where a principal like Jack Webb in Dragnet says, 'Just the facts, ma'am.' "

What is clear from caring organizations is that the context in which values are articulated is as important as the message. Continuity between words and actions is fundamental. Equally essential is respect for the role that young people must play in receiving and processing what the organization seeks to convey. Tim Parent of Smokey House explained, "In a relationship built on mutual respect, lectures and judgements aren't going to be very effective . . . We try to set out standards and explain as clearly as possible why they're important . . . But finally buying into the value is up to them."

Supporting Staff

The "burnout" that many experience in social service professions has been the subject of much research.[5] Chapter 3 discussed how boundaries and distancing can help youth workers prevent burnout; but another strategy is to enhance and support workers' resources through norms of mutual caregiving and systems of support for staff. An organization can support mutual caregiving by fostering relationships among staff—through regular team-building activities, for example. Caregiving practices can also be modeled in supervisors' styles. At The Warming House, several staff members spoke of the executive director's care for them as integral to their ability to care for youths. At Smokey House, Lynn Bondurant has encouraged staff to speak with her when they are looking for other jobs and made it clear that no one will be penalized for openly exploring other job options.

Systems of support also involve specific structures or practices. At Smokey House, considerable training time is spent explaining that "they don't have to do this alone—that nobody's going to look down at them and say, 'Bad you, you couldn't do it yourself,'" said Lynn Bondurant. Crew leaders, foremen, and the crew and educational coordinators meet every morning for ten minutes and for half an hour at the end of each day. These are times to discuss mundane issues of planning, as well as to share particular problems and ask for help. Less experienced staff are told that every question is okay, "and I think some of the more experienced staff make a point of asking some really stupid questions just to show them it's okay," laughed Lynn. At The Warming House, the staff meet regularly to discuss particular individuals and staffs' reactions to them, with the goal of helping staff members interact more effectively with problem youths. The Block Brothers get together every Saturday morning for two hours to talk about the coming week's schedule, and each Block Brother is expected to talk about his greatest challenges of the week. "I try to talk the least," said Nate Smith, the Block Brothers Director, "so that the guys can come to look to each other for ideas and solutions."

Structures that offer staff autonomy, flexibility, and input can give staff greater feelings of empowerment and thus greater job satisfaction.[6] Many of these practices involve seeing the organization as having a role in supporting staff members' growth and helping them balance work and other obligations. Smokey House expects crew leaders to budget and plan for their areas and builds up a Center-wide plan from this information. Despite limited resources, the Center provides funds for staff to take relevant college courses. The Center has also made it comfortable for staff to bring their children to work whenever possible. El Puente pairs new facilitators with more senior staff for team teaching and mentoring, and also immediately makes them part of the committees responsible for setting school policies. "You're brought into a family right away. . . . you're given power . . . and people want to hear from you," explained Hector Calderòn. "You're integrated into different communities . . . not treated as, 'Well, you just got here, you'd better wait your turn.'"

Meeting Needs for Belonging

Schools and other organized care providers can consciously facilitate a young person's attachment to their organizations through traditions, rituals, and other practices that celebrate the young person's involvement and reciprocate his enthusiasm. "You have to give people opportunities to express their feelings for the group; to reaffirm their belonging," explained Luis Garden Acosta of El Puente. At the end of every season at Smokey House, young people participate in a formal graduation and receive a variety of awards and certificates for their efforts. Each season produces a yearbook; "we're always taking pictures for the yearbook and we give as many as possible away to the kids," said Lynn Bondurant.

Team-building is another practice that supports feelings of belonging and attachment. Smokey House began issuing color-coded t-shirts to different crews a few years ago and found that it made an enormous difference to the youths. Tim Parent explained,

> Kids started saying, "I'm on the green team" or "I was on the red team." I had never heard them actually say team before. They had never thought of themselves as a group initially, but this gave them a sense of identity—on the first day they had visible signs that they belonged.

Young Native American youths attending the NIYLP summer camp are organized into clans in which they play, sleep, and do assigned chores. The clans are based on Native American tradition, but at the camp they are meant as a way of giving young people a smaller group with which to relate and a chance to build relationships with people of different ages and tribes.

In caring organizations, team building is as intentional as all other practices.

"There's an ideal mix of 'good' kids and troubled kids, of kids that can be role models and kids that need to be brought along," explained Mac Hall of NIYLP. At Smokey House, assigning young people to crews is a laborious process that involves taking into account their stated choices as well as their developmental needs. As a coed work environment, Smokey House has struggled with the pros and cons of dividing groups equally among boys and girls. "Sometimes you have kid that really needs a male or female role model, and that should come first," said Lynn Bondurant. Some crew leaders believe that mixed-gender crews are more difficult to manage, while others find single-sex crews more fractious. The Center has also found that young women sometimes have a better experience on all-female crews. Regardless of their specific grouping strategy, all of these organizations think carefully about how to group the young people in their programs.

Attention to belonging also requires careful management of transitions. Demonstrating sensitivity to departures—both each day and at the end of a young person's tenure—helps young people attach to an organization and the people in it. On a daily basis, such customs as Tim Parent greeting the school-bus and the ten minutes of free, "transition" time granted the youth workers every afternoon at Smokey House are ways organizations can show young people that they are understood as individuals who have lives outside of the organization. Intentional management of graduations and other forms of leave-taking demonstrate that the relationship the young person has built with the organization, as well as with its members, is important enough to commemorate, and that the development the young person has experienced while affiliated with the organization is important enough to celebrate. Organizations have differing philosophies of termination: The Warming House believes that graduation requires a complete termination of relationships between staff and youths, while Smokey House Center has experimented with mentoring young people in their next employment situation; but marking leave-taking with ceremony appears to be a hallmark of caring organizations.

Opening Up Lines of Communication

Organizations can facilitate effective caregiving and encourage relationship building among both youths and staff by creating an atmosphere in which communication in all directions is encouraged. Some of this practice may be management style—many caring organizations are run by directors who maintain an "open door" for staff and young people alike—but institutionalized practices can also contribute to this climate. Smokey House runs circle meetings weekly, and more often in response to particular problems. The meetings are meant to keep crews informed of each other's activities and build cohesion and identity among the Center at large; they are also a way, as Lynn Bondurant explained, "to model problem solving in which everyone participates in a constructive, nonadversarial process."

Building a culture in which everyone is accessible also requires structuring teams and groups flexibly enough that individuals can form relationships across groups as well as within them. The Block Brothers see part of their job as shepherding their charges toward available mentors who share their interests and can meet their needs. As one Block Brother explained,

> We all offer something different, so if one of my kids wants to run, I am not going to say no, you have to do art instead; I'll call up [another Block Brother] and say I got a kid who wants to practice with you. We don't have the mentality where we are fighting for each other's kids . . . We all have different talents. Kevin may be able to handle a situation with my kid that I am not able to handle; I am man enough to say that he should go to talk to Kevin because I don't know what to do.

At Smokey House, youths rarely spend two seasons under the supervision of the same crew leader. Center-wide events, such as camping trips and volleyball games, are opportunities to work in different teams and get to know other staff and youths.

El Puente has developed a variety of extracurricular activities that allow multiple opportunities for students to interact with facilitators outside of class, as well as with students from other grades. In addition to the many special events and after-school activities, the Academy also devotes school time to town meetings, support circles of facilitators and students from different grades, and mentoring programs. These activities are opportunities for staff to hear, and sense, how well they are doing with young people.

Many of El Puente's nonacademic meetings are also explicitly oriented toward discussion of personal, emotional responses to issues of importance to youth. The school periodically holds meetings called Sacred Circles that involve the entire El Puente community. Usually convened in response to a crisis or important occasion, these meetings are oriented toward deep emotions and deep convictions. Allowing youths to access this level of communication, Frances Lucerna believes, is part of what makes El Puente a special place for young people: "Really talking about that which . . . makes the core of a human being . . . I think it is probably the most powerful part of being here at El Puente for young people . . . that the facilitators have designed time for young people and adults to come together to experience that which is deep within one's self."

Perhaps the single greatest factor in open communication is what one young person at Smokey House called "letting your normal self out." Communication and relationship building are facilitated in organizations in which staff feel free to act and relate as individuals outside of their professional roles. These are places that are safe for both young people and the adults who work with them. They are places where staff, as well as youths, feel accepted, valued, and listened to.

Keeping Clear Vision

Sustaining the spirit of a caring school or other organization requires ongoing effort: attention to the messages sent by each decision or action, training of new staff and youth members, and the endless process of attentiveness, responsiveness, and competence that characterizes care. Staff and management of caring organizations devote a lot of time to this effort and are likely, when they talk about how they spend their day, to describe themselves as conferring with colleagues and meeting with youths in both planned and spontaneous encounters. Caring organizations understand that the climate they have created in their environment is special, and they are willing to allocate the staff time needed to maintain it.

While this commitment to the process of caring originates at the top of an organization, caring survives because the commitment is accepted at all levels. Here again, hiring and acculturation are critical. "People on the outside look at us and say, 'Gosh, that must be so much work,' " said Lynn Bondurant of Smokey House. "But for us, it feels easy, in part because once you've established it, the people who come here expect this climate."

Sustaining a caring organization also demands vigilant focus on one's mission. "In youth programming, with so many different funding streams, it's easy to get schizophrenic," said Lynn Bondurant. "In everything we plan, we try to begin and end with the same question: 'Is this what we want for our kids?' "

REACHING BEYOND THE WALLS: PRACTICES THAT CREATE CONNECTIONS IN YOUNG PEOPLE'S LIVES

Most schools and organizations recognize that their influence on a young person is constrained by the extent that other important forces on a young person's life—family, community, and peer group—support and reflect values consistent with those the organizations is trying to promote. An important characteristic of caring organizations is their institutional attention to and concern for the entirety of an individual's situation. These organizations actively seek to transfer the practices of care that are effective in their settings to other institutions in which young people participate. They are also teaching the values of holism, and the connections between face-to-face caring and social action, to the youths in their care. Organizations practice this value in a number of ways: by promoting norms and expectations for communication across interested parties, through programs designed to explore and celebrate culture, and by enabling interaction between home, community, school, and other institutions important to a young person's life. In contrast to the practices described in the previous section, many of these efforts are conscious attempts to move beyond the internal functions of the organization to the larger context of a young person's life.

Celebrating Culture

Acknowledgment and celebration of culture can be a context in which to express caring. Activities organized around culturally specific events lend an intimacy and a purpose to gatherings, allowing young people to share the practices and rituals of their families with peers and encouraging young people to explore the messages embedded in the culture. NIYLP embodies this approach most explicitly, bringing the young people involved in its summer camp and school-year programs to local homes for the elderly for instruction in Native American practices and philosophies. El Puente holds several special events a year drawn from Latino heritage as well as from the Caribbean, African American, and other cultures of students and staff.

Connections to a young person's cultural practices and expectations help to create the structures that undergird caring. NIYLP has drawn on the strong tradition of the servant leader in Native American culture to create a service learning program that is philosophically and ethically supported by its connections to Native American practices. El Puente has a formal mentorship program that draws on the Latino tradition of godparents, unrelated adults who have sacred and powerful roles in a person's life. In some cases, the cultural connections can be unplanned and unanticipated. "I didn't grow up in a traditional Navajo family, so I don't think of myself as consciously bringing that cultural connection to the kids," said Andrea Tsosie, a youth worker with NIYLP of Navajo descent. "But then I find that when I want to make a point, I tell a story—that's a very traditional way to connect."

Particularly for minority youths, the acknowledgment that their differences from the majority culture are worthy of celebration rather than suppression can be an expression of care in and of itself. The task of helping a young person to respect his culture, and thereby himself, is a multifaceted effort. Programs and associations that are organized around cultural specifics implicitly validate and celebrate the culture. They are also institutionalized evidence that a young person belongs to something that has continuity and value to others.

Fostering Relationships

For many youth organizations, parental support of their children's involvement and, importantly, understanding and acceptance of the organization's values and practices is crucial to success with a young person. Connections to teachers and others important to a young person's life are similarly important. Caring schools and other organizations develop relationships with parents and others that can open up lines of communication in times of crisis and help to reinforce messages and guidance that the organization is trying to transmit. Block Brothers make a point of meeting parents early in the school year, and visiting their group members' homes so that the parents feel the Brothers are a resource to them as well as to their children. Smokey House schedules a formal visit to each new worker's family to review the expectations the Center holds for its youth, and provides a handbook of policies and practices. Because many of the parents of NIYLP's students are sensitive to cultural issues—some do not want their children exposed to any native culture, while others are wary of the culture being treated disrespectfully—NIYLP staff contact and sound out parents about their boundaries for their children on issues relating to religion and native culture.

Research on the impact of parent involvement in school on their children's performance has shown that connections between at-home and out-of-home care can have powerful effects. Countless research studies have found that parents who participate in school activities, show interest in their children's schoolwork, and convey high aspirations for their children's education have unequivocally positive effects on their children's school performance.[7] As parents support schooling, schools can also support parenting: parents who have participated in demonstration projects in schools that offer a forum in which to get together and discuss their common concerns have reported that such experiences have helped them with their relationships with their children and with their parenting skills.[8] Organizations can become more effective caregivers and can promote caring in other areas of the lives of youth they serve by fostering relationships and encouraging involvement and communication.

Reaching out to families, communities, and other organizations is also a way in which schools and other organizations can model responsible citizenry to the young people they serve. Organizations that involve themselves in issues of concern to their community can help create meaningful civic roles for their youth members. Even if young people choose not to participate, such organizational commitment transmits messages about the value of service and social action. Outreach to other institutions in the community can also, quite simply, normalize traditionally tense relationships and reduce some of the isolation many adolescents feel in their own communities. The Warming House has made it a policy to invite members of the local police force to the center and to volunteer for service projects at the police station. "Most of our kids wouldn't encounter the police unless they'd done something bad," explained Cindy Nash. "But now, the policemen always drop by, and they [the police] know all our kids."

Promoting the Development of Parents, Teachers, and the Community

Although schools and other youth organizations clearly are oriented toward promoting the development of the young people they serve, many have found the development of others influential in a young person's life to be a natural consequence, and sometimes a necessary component, of their primary mission. Smokey House has found that its process of constructive discipline can be developmental for parents as well as for youths. Because it is located in a rural area, Smokey House runs a bus to bring its young workers from school to the Center and back home. Each student pays $1.00 a day for the service, a fraction of the actual cost, but enough so that the young person takes some responsibility for his transportation. Misbehavior on the bus is not uncommon; when it occurs, a young person gets a warning, then a second warning, and then parents are asked to be involved. As Lynn Bondurant explained, Smokey House's disciplinary process can be a learning experience for parents:

> ... almost inevitably when the time comes that we say, I am sorry but you cannot be on the bus, the parent will call ... we often have parents who don't have very good skills, who don't understand that it is important to be involved all along; they haven't expressed to their kids ... [that] there will be ramifications to your actions. So instead what happens is the parent steps in and says you can't do that to my kids, my child is entitled to that. And we have to say, actually the school pays for the program, but we pay for the bus ... and it is not very pleasant ... If we were to say that the young person can never ever ride the bus again, I think the learning process would stop, so instead we sit down with the parent and the child ... and they say, well, one more chance, and we say no, that is what we did in the first place, but if the young person can find another way to work for, say, six weeks and talk about what they could do at

school or at home to demonstrate during those six weeks that they now have control of this, and then they can request to ride the bus again. We set it up that way so that maybe the parent finally kicks in and says, 'Oh boy, this is affecting me' . . . it is a painstakingly slow process, but it can happen. So it is not just developmental for the young person, but for the parent too, they have to realize that there is a line here and I can't just make a lot of noise like I do at the public school and they back right down . . . sometimes the parent, like the child, has to test that line.

Many organizations have made the development of other members of the community a programmatic priority. Smokey House runs a summer training program for teachers from many of the schools its workers attend. El Puente has organized its school around the themes of social justice it promotes in community organizing and public health activities. NIYLP provides technical assistance to school districts in Native American areas that wish to develop traditionally based service learning programs for their students.

In many cases, the relationships built through organizational efforts serve to increase communication between parents, youth workers, teachers, and other members of the community. Strengthening social bonds in this way can build trust in a community that can spill into areas beyond any individual youth. A study of the impact of newly established Boys and Girls Clubs in public housing developments found that the process of establishing and managing the clubs stimulated communication between public housing residents, the police, housing authority management, and other community groups. The increased communication improved the safety and enriched the social life of the public housing development. This improved environment, in turn, positively affected the development of all children and adolescents in the developments.[9]

El Puente is unique in that its school is an outgrowth of the community development work it has been pursuing for decades. To Luis Garden Acosta, El Puente's founder, creating a caring school and promoting social justice through community organizing are but two facets of the same activity:

If we start with the realization that as human beings we are naturally interdependent, then to the extent that we create community we are human . . . and the building block of community is the exercise of love and caring. . . . Working for social justice is working to allow people to express their humanity, to live humanely. . . . Our primary task here [at the school] is to develop young people as human beings . . . and in [community organizing] it is similarly to develop community, to make our community more human . . . Every minute spent to liberate the minds of our young people and our community is a minute spent in the pursuit of social justice.

Caring within organizations is but one step in the development of a caring, socially cohesive culture. There is important work to be done to extend caring into communities and society at large. The next chapter will address this task.

CHAPTER 7

Building a Caring Community

This afternoon is the annual summer picnic and prayer meeting at Oak Knoll Apartments, a low-income housing development in Gary, Indiana, that is owned by the Tree of Life Community Development Corporation. Young people from the Tree of Life Missionary Baptist Church have been moving tables and gathering supplies since early morning. Men, women, and children in the purple t-shirts that are Tree of Life's unofficial uniform mill about, while others visit inside townhomes where doors are open wide and crowds are in kitchens. Oak Knoll itself looks more like a suburban condominium development than public housing. Tree of Life Community Development Corporation bought the complex from the Department of Housing and Urban Development for a dollar two years ago, and then took out an $11 million loan to refurbish it. A new tenants' center features a large, immaculate laundry room, as well as a social center and meeting rooms where residents can meet with counselors and social workers employed by Tree of Life. The only reminder that this is the inner city is around the back, where workers are busy repairing a unit riddled with bullet holes.

There are many young people in attendance—perhaps 70 percent of those present are under eighteen—but Dr. Cato Brooks Jr., Senior Pastor of the Tree of Life Missionary Baptist Church, said, "We don't focus on youth programming per se. Young people are involved in every aspect of our ministry: they are teaching, singing in the choir, mentoring, preaching, working in the community . . . We teach our young people; we don't have them play kiddie games." Tree of Life's philosophy is that the best program for a young person is one that works to improve her entire environment.

Pastor Brooks and his wife, Betty, founded Tree of Life Missionary Baptist

Church in 1979 in an abandoned building in inner-city Gary. The couple's mission to rebuild this community is inspired, motivated, and, Pastor Brooks would say, dictated by their religious faith. "The Lord gathered me to Chicago, and then to here," said Pastor Brooks. "To me it is a perfect opportunity given to us by God to do something in this city. . . That is my only reason for being here." The church has since rebuilt that structure and established seven missions and seventeen house churches in surrounding neighborhoods.

The church is a crowded place on Sundays—several hundred come to worship—but during the week almost all activity takes place elsewhere. "We are together as a church five days a week, but we only need to be in the church for Sunday School and services," explained Pastor Brooks. "The rest of the week we are in the community." The Ministry runs missions in housing projects; counsels juvenile offenders at school and at home; and staffs outreach programs that offer family counseling, material assistance, and social support to families struggling in the inner city. The aim is not to bring people into the church on Sundays, but to bring the church community into their lives all week.

'To be a pastor in the inner city, you must be more than a preacher," said Pastor Brooks. "I believe God has given us this part of Gary to revitalize, and I mean that in every respect: spiritually, materially, socially."

To that end, Tree of Life has embarked on a comprehensive, spiritually and economically based effort to change the lives of families in inner-city Gary. Although the mission is spiritually inspired, it is very much based in the community. Tree of Life's religious vision motivates and shapes its mission, allowing its members clarity and continuity between streets and church. Pastor Brooks explained:

> In Sunday School we talk about the Lord and His Scriptures, in the community we talk about community. [Many organizations] separate the two so that there is a difference in coming to church and feeling one way and going home and feeling another way; but it should be the *same* feeling . . . That is why we do the outreach.

An important part of Tree of Life's mission is developing an economic base for the community that can offer employment and self-sufficiency for all residents and role models for youth. In 1991, Tree of Life formed a community development corporation to own and manage commercial operations. In addition to owning and operating Oak Knoll, the CDC is considering investments in shopping malls and other real estate. Tree of Life Community Development Corporation has also become a large social service provider, with contracts from state and local government to work with juvenile delinquents, families in crisis, and substance abuse prevention.

At Tree of Life, youth development is seen in the context of family and community development. Programming for young people in isolation of this larger mission "is a waste of time," declared Pastor Brooks. "Young people are not the problem, they are the victims. If we concentrate solely on them we are treating the symptoms and not the cause." Large-scale, sustainable improvement in the prospects for young people comes only with economic, social, and spiritual development of the entire community. Youth development, then, is as much about "understanding why we would invest millions of dollars in a housing project . . . so that they will have something" as it is about mentoring programs. "I want to give them choices," said Pastor Brooks, "real choices, and then show them the benefits of making the right ones."

At Tree of Life, helping young people make the right choices is a process that involves a comprehensive social network to express love and care. Like most communities of faith, Tree of Life is staffed primarily by volunteers. The Church has only three employees, including Pastor Brooks; some church members have jobs at the community development corporation, but the vast majority are employed elsewhere and volunteer their time to the church community. One of the most important volunteer jobs is as a youth counselor, responsible for a dozen or so young people ages 13 to 18 in the church community. The counselors meet with their charges individually and in groups both at church and at the counselor's home in sessions that are understood to be entirely confidential. Although the counselors are carefully selected—most are older people with grown children, "there is no great philosophy surrounding this practice," said Pastor Brooks. "It's really no different than what you'd do with your own children." Pastor Brooks himself takes pride in personally checking every child's report card, going to every graduation, and attending parent-teacher conferences when necessary.

Many other youths have found special mentoring relationships in the context of the church. Lisa, age 15, started coming to Tree of Life about two years ago while struggling with her parents' divorce. She's since developed a relationship with Pastor Brooks' adult daughter, whom she visits on her own "when I have problems. I'm glad she's there," said Lisa, "because I have trouble talking to some people and I can talk to her."

While the counselors have structured "rap" sessions, a lot of the learning, like the relationships, is informal. "You kind of pick up on what other people are doing, especially the love," one young man said.

At Tree of Life, the youth experience fits seamlessly into the activities of the larger community. Young people are neither segregated nor treated as miniature adults; caring adults support their development while expecting that they will contribute meaningfully to the community. Youths are expected to take on adult roles in church operations, including teaching in Sunday School, working as a nurse, serving breakfast to the younger children on Sunday mornings, and helping out in neighborhood programs. "They make decisions, they are part of our Church council, we ask them for advice," said Pastor Brooks. "We don't deal with our young people as the future, we deal with them as our present."

At the block party, many of the young people head off for a volleyball game, while others play with little children and hang out in kitchens and living rooms. About an hour into the party, children and adults begin to gather on the grass in front of a microphone and a pair of speakers, and Deion, 16, begins to preach. His voice has the familiar cadence of Southern Baptist preachers, and he speaks with assurance: he's done this before. He is also speaking to friends; many of the group are young people who have come out to support him. Deion is followed by three more young men, all under twenty, who are part of the more than twenty-five young men training to be reverends with Pastor Brooks.

Deion has been coming to Tree of Life since he was small, and he has grown up in a community of youths surrounded and supported by a community of adults. "At school, you receive encouragement, but there is a lot of negativity . . . at church you know somebody will pick you up if you need it, and there is always a hand on your back, and you always feel it there." Youths receive encouragement not only from Pastor Brooks but from the entire church community. Adults at church, says Deion, "come up to you, say, 'Man, I am so proud of you, I heard you were in such and such, and I am going to come see you, I am going to let everybody know' . . . so you know it is real."

The church is also the context for this group of young people's social life. "We all grew up together," says George, 18, an associate pastor who will leave for college in the fall. "We go spend the night at each others' houses, we are used to spending all our time together." Tree of Life has a large youth group and youth choir, "and is just full of love, honestly," said Synita, a young woman of 20. "When a young person comes to our church, all of us go out and introduce ourselves, we make the person feel welcome . . . we invite the person out with us after church."

Like the adults in their community, the young people at Tree of Life speak with absolute assurance and conviction about their mission. They know exactly what their organization is doing and why. Deion described his primary work thus:

> the main thing with the young people is to get them involved while they are
> young. So we are trying to get them involved and let them know right up

front who God is, and that this is a serious thing, we are not here to play games. And we let them know that everybody has an eternity and it is either going to be Heaven or Hell and they have to choose which they want.

Regardless of one's personal religious views, the power of these young people's values cannot be debated. Tree of Life's mission is so powerful precisely because it is comprehensive, addressing all aspects of their lives, and clearly focused on the situation of those in its community. Its strength comes in its unified vision of an individual's role with respect to self, family, church, and community. It is, ultimately, about translating one's love of God into actions that express love and care for individuals and for the community. As Pastor Brooks explained,

> We want them [young people] to know that every privilege brings a responsibility . . . Freedom is to do what you should. That is how we define it: freedom is the ability to do what needs to be done and should be done, before you do what you want to do.

*   *   *

There are "rational" explanations for why people extend themselves to care for others, but such explanations often fall short. Western philosophical thought, dominated as it is by notions of ego, control, and self-interest, has generally regarded care as a mechanism of genetic survival or a means of social exchange. Utility theory, with its focus on preference and utility, has offered a framework for interpreting social relations in terms of market relations. Yet describing care as a biological impulse or the calculated response of a rational choice model of thought misses some of its most essential features: its role as an expression of values and the way it is understood by caregivers.

Care is a socially constructed concept that is created from what we imagine ourselves to be capable of. It is shaped by our understanding of our value as human beings and of the potential inherent in social interaction. It is neither scientific nor purely rational: what we think is true goes a longer way to explaining our behavior than what might, in a purely objective view, be deemed factual.

What we believe about care is crucially important. Having a clear definition of care can serve as a motivator for prosocial action. In his ambitious study of caring behaviors in America, *Acts of Compassion*, the sociologist Robert Wuthnow examined both the prevalence and practice of care in our society and people's explanations of why they did what they did. He argues that people's access to the very concept of the existence of care, whether through religious beliefs, social values, or views of human nature, goes a long way toward explaining why they act in caring manners. Wuthnow speaks explicitly about the importance of the discourse in which caring behavior is described: "Our ability to care may not depend on giving one account rather than another. But being able to give some account makes it possible to conceive of our behaviors as caring."

Chapter 1 explained how naming is itself a process that empowers individuals to action and understanding. The philosopher Charles Taylor has described how articulating notions of "the good" helps to create "moral sources" that serve as organizers and motivators of social action. Moral sources, as Taylor describes them, are a means of understanding our actions by reference to shared, articulated values.[2] One of the reasons the members of Tree of Life form such a powerful community is that they share and can articulate a firm moral source that has meaning for their lives. Moral sources do not have to refer to God, or even to be religious in any sense. They do, however, imply values.

This chapter will explore how care is extended beyond face-to-face acts and the actions of individual institutions to the community at large. Is there a way to think about our roles as caregivers that forms a cohesive picture of our relations with intimate others, with community members, and with the institutions and organizations that comprise our society? Are there "moral sources" that can help us understand and express our responsibilities to fellow citizens and society at large? What kinds of structures and supports are necessary so that individuals can help to care for large-scale social systems?

These questions cannot be addressed without considering trust, a theme that has been explored in previous chapters with respect to its role in developing an individual's capacity to care. Just as trust is foundational to individual capacity, it is elemental to caring in social systems. Again, how we understand the reasons and mechanisms by which people trust goes a long way toward describing what we believe is possible in society. If we believe that trust is solely a rational calculus of market exchange, we are not likely to extend it very far. If, however, we see trust as a "moral source," we grant it value apart from its role in any individual interaction. Such value can accrue to institutions and social structures as well as to individuals: public trust can be established as an end in and of itself. This frame of mind is essential to a caring society.

Public trust, however, is a fragile concept, and it is easier to document its demise than to explain its creation. The final section of this chapter will consider the challenges to creating and sustaining public trust and care across groups. Some barriers are structural: caring is often about belonging, but belonging implies exclusion. How does one maintain the benefits of belonging without teaching or practicing exclusion, intolerance, or extended self-interest? Likewise, the differences between us are often barriers to understanding and thereby to trust and caring. How does one reach across groups competently?

Some of the other challenges to promoting caring in larger social systems are not structural, but perceptual. These challenges relate to our perceptions of what is relevant to public and to private life, as well as to what is "women's work" and where children belong. We have restricted caring to the private sphere, and so have made it difficult to create a role for caring in the public sphere. Many aspects of culture express a notion of "the good" that focuses on personal satisfaction, spontaneity, and self-fulfillment. Such messages inhibit care in society by undermining the values of community and interdependence upon which care rests.

The work required to address these sorts of challenges involves articulating new ways of viewing the world and exploring how to promote and support caring values across society. Many of these challenges are attitudinal; and changing attitudes, like changing culture, is a slow and laborious process. Promoting caring across society is, finally, subversive: it requires us to challenge assumptions of how people act and of what is valuable in life.

EXTENDING THE PRACTICE OF CARE

At the beginning of this book, a four-part typology of caring was presented to explain the many circumstances and ways of caring. The typology encompasses spontaneous, face-to-face acts of care, care provided in a professional context, care facilitated and supported by organizations, and finally the ways in which an entire society can be caring. Although this typology describes larger and larger systems of care, at every level it is individuals who practice the attentiveness, responsiveness, and competence that comprise caring behaviors. What motivates individuals to care in circumstances outside their immediate context? What venues are available to care for strangers and those not immediately accessible? How do people show care for institutions and for their community or country?

It is fairly easy to describe the way people care in spontaneous, face-to-face acts of caring. This type of caring includes care for friends and family as well as care for the self.[3] The philosopher and educator Nel Noddings has described an individual's "map" of caring activity as a set of concentric circles in which one's commitment, like the circles created by a stone thrown in the water, becomes less intense and more diffuse as one moves away from those to whom one is closest.[4] Such a set of circles can be envisioned as a quasi-physical arrangement, organized around the self and our social relationships to other individuals. We would expect that one's spouse and children come first; then relatives, friends, neighbors, and members of our "group," until care is a vague and diffuse concept involving strangers with no relation to us.

Professor Noddings's map of caring works quite well to explain how individuals participate in face-to-face care, but it does not cover the entire range of caregiving activities. We rarely need to talk of principle in explaining why we care for our children, for example; for most of us, it is a natural reaction that we experience as more emotional than principled. But other forms of care, such as volunteering in a soup kitchen, reaching out to a troubled youth, or organizing a get-out-the-vote campaign in one's community, often spring more from principles than from an immediate emotional response. A map of those around us does not explain how people practice care based on principle, or in the context of their professional lives. It also does not explain how people actively care for causes, institutions, and other social systems that affect them in more and less immediate ways. An additional dimension of organization is necessary to describe the practice of care in these more abstract, less immediate contexts. One can imagine a second set of concentric circles that would, of course, interact with the first; but existing on a more abstract, principled plane. The second set of circles could be thought of as a *moral cosmos* in which one organizes his ideals and values according to his personal views of their importance. The moral cosmos does not refer to a type of care that is less active than that demonstrated in Professor Noddings's "map." Rather, it is a way of organizing caring actions that arise from principles or moral sources.

Caring for systems—for an organization, a community, or a cause—is as rigorous and concrete as caring for individuals. System-level care, like face-to-face caring, can be held to similar standards of constancy, devotion, and practice. The same distinction between caring for—active caring—and caring about can be made. Just as the practice of caring for individuals must involve active extension of self in tangible forms, so too caring about systems requires that one engage in active behaviors to sustain the systems or effect the changes in which one believes.

There is no denying that it is harder to care actively in one's moral cosmos than in the circles that define our everyday lives. Unlike families, organizations and systems have goals that are often vague and usually broader than the capacities of a single individual. There are not always prescribed roles to play in collective efforts, and when there are roles, one is less likely to find guidance from elders or peers in how to perform in them. Moreover, the demands of work and family often leave little sustained attention for "extracurricular" activities, making it all too difficult to muster the responsiveness needed to care effectively.

Organized care settings—not only those devoted to the care of young people—can help individuals care for others outside of their immediate social sphere, as well as for causes in which they believe. By supporting, sponsoring, and engaging in organizations—such as churches, neighborhood clubs, and regional or national causes—we extend ourselves beyond immediate face-to-face care to the care for those groups and causes that we believe are our responsibility. Organized care is a way to share the caring roles and actions for both our own children and for the groups, causes, and systems we wish to support. It allows us to offer those for whom we care specialized services that we might not be able to provide as individuals, and allows us to participate, albeit indirectly, in the care of others whom we do not know personally but whose situations are important in our moral cosmos.

Organized care providers are a form of the "mediating structures" that sociologists argue provide much of the cohesion and continuity in our lives. The sociologist Peter Berger describes mediating structures as "those institutions standing between the individual in his private life and the large institutions of public life."[5] These are institutions—such as the family, church, neighborhood, and voluntary associations—that mediate between the spheres of private life and the bureaucratic institutions that control most of public life, including government, economic enterprise, education, and organized professions. In Berger's analysis, these mediating structures are the means by which individuals achieve stability in their private lives and meaning in their public lives. They are particular and personal enough to provide meaning and identity for individual existence, and yet organized enough to offer the individual support and access to the larger society.

Our participation in these mediating structures, then, is a way of extending ourselves beyond direct care for intimate others to express care for both values and for people we do not know. It is also a means to receive care that our intimates are either unable or unavailable to provide in a forum that is still personal and connected to the particularities of our unique lives. Mediating structures are shaped from and respond to the values and realities of the people who create them. They offer a public form of care, but one that is collective and voluntary, rather than coercive and bureaucratic.

Organized care might be voluntary, but this fact does not imply that it is not essential. Historically, organized care has served as a social safety net in the lives of the children and families who participate in it. In many cases, the care provided by mediating structures is redundant with that offered in primary, direct caregiving situations. Such redundancy protects against the temporary or long-term failure of the primary care system. A system of multiple sources of organized care such as found in a large, extended family in a healthy community serves as a safety net of care for the smallest social units.

Because they are "ground-up" institutions, created and sustained by the citizens who support them, organized care providers can offer care of children that is complementary, and not compensatory, to their primary, direct care. Organized care can be a be privately organized—but publicly supported—

means by which the efforts of primary caregivers are extended and enhanced in a consonant manner.

The concept of organized care is a bridge from face-to-face care to the social construction of care throughout society. A notion of organized care allows us to consider how care is practiced outside of the private sphere of family and close relationships. It is a way of conceptualizing the broad range of social structures and institutions upon which we rely for much of the contextual support of our social interactions. By expanding a notion of care outside the realm of active, interpersonal relations in the private sphere, we can begin to consider a broad range of caring opportunities and situations. We can consider whether organized caring is, or is not, taking place; we can consider how it is distributed throughout our social systems; and we can examine how it is or is not effectively demonstrated.

TRUST AS A MORAL SOURCE

Chapter 3 described how the trust an infant develops in his primary caregiver is the foundation of healthy social development. From consistent, appropriate attendance to his basic needs the infant learns to trust his caregiver, himself, and finally the world. In Erik Erikson's view, the successful resolution of the task of developing trust allows one to move forward to build new capabilities, including, most importantly, the ability to care for and nurture a future generation. In this way, care and trust are linked in a chicken-and-egg sort of way: caring fosters trust, which leads to caring, which fosters trust in the next generation.

Trust and care are similarly linked in individual relationships throughout the life cycle. Trust is foundational in all interpersonal relations, in that it is the basis for forming expectations of the behavior of others and the likely consequences of actions. Caring relationships, in particular, rely on trust to establish norms of mutuality and responsiveness. It is trust that allows young people to feel safe in caring youth programs, trust that facilitates the exposure of their vulnerable selves to peers and adults.

The role of trust in social exchange has been most fully explored in scholarship concerning social capital. Social capital is a property of the relations between individuals that facilitates communication, collective action, and the maintenance of social norms. Theories of social capital have considered trust as a product of rational choice about the long-term benefits of keeping one's word or meeting expectations in a particular instance. This is trust as a social contract, in which trust is viewed as an instrument of efficient social exchanges. In this contractual model of trust, trust is motivated by an expectation of the material benefits of ongoing interactions.[6] A contractual view of trust would expect the bonds of trust to be determined by a rational calculation of the likelihood of future interactions and the ability to enforce repercussions of breaches of trust. A famous example of this conception of trust is the diamond merchants of New York City, who regularly transfer extremely valuable diamonds among themselves with no documentation and no checks to ensure that an inferior diamond is not substituted for the original upon return. Trust is high in this network, according to the contractual view of trust, because the merchants have frequent, ongoing exchanges and because the merchants come from a closed social group that not only works together but lives together, prays together, and intermarries, so that the consequences of a violation of trust would be manifold.[7]

However, contractual models such as the above example are inadequate to explain people's trust in others. The feelings people have about each other and about society at large might be far more important in explaining their trusting behaviors than the benefits they derive from shared trust. Research has found, for example, that there are noninstrumental motivations to trust, particularly relational issues such as identification with an individual or a group, affective processes, and feelings of moral obligation to others.[8] Such evidence suggests that trust might have a social meaning beyond that proposed by rational calculations. People might trust and allow others to trust them because they value trustworthiness as an attribute of the larger society. In other words, trust might be motivated by the belief that social trust is a shared public good that one is morally obligated to protect. In this perspective, social trust is practically an entity in itself, a moral force that can make claims upon the actions of individuals.

A vision of trust as a "moral source" is essential to a caring society. It can be the moral authority from which collectives, including voluntary associations and civic entities, hold expectations of their members or citizens. Like the moral sources upon which the Tree of Life community draws, trust bespeaks the responsibilities of individuals to their group, community, or country. When citizens accept the moral force that holds them responsible to their community, they are not conceptualizing their responsibilities in terms of a rational exchange for any rights or benefits that might accrue to them as citizens. Their acceptance of the notion that their community has the moral authority to hold expectations of them comes from their belief in the value of a trusting society. Thus, just as trust is foundational to caring in individual relationships, so too can it be seen as the basis for citizenship in a participatory, caring democracy.

What is the source of this immensely valuable quality? It is relatively easy to plot the development of trust between two people: a history of positive interactions, combined with a growing sense of mutual respect and affection, creates the expectation that one can trust the other to care for her, or for what she cares about, consistently and competently. The development of trust in organizations or large-scale social systems, however, is more complicated. Because they are large and complex, such groups often do not offer individuals opportunities for repeated interchanges.[9] Moreover, the high possibility of one's isolated acts of trustworthiness being lost in a sea of indifference diminishes one's motivation to make efforts to act responsibly. Whereas in individual relationships one can "size up" another and determine whether it is prudent to trust him, the facelessness of larger structures means that one is unable to gauge the risks of trusting. Without recourse to individual relationships, a person must find a principled, emotional, or reasoned motivation—or some combination of all three—to trust others and behave in a trustworthy manner himself.

When he first came to Gary, Indiana, Pastor Brooks explained, he found "people who were disillusioned, who had been betrayed by those they had put their trust in. There was not much hope." Building trust, he believes, is the first step toward reaching out to members of the community and helping them become engaged in Tree of Life's mission. Pastor Brooks's focus on trust influences many details large and small in his mission, including how he dresses and what kind of car he drives. But fundamentally, building trust is a long-term, gradual process of consistency and commitment. An institution builds trust in a community, according to Pastor Brooks,

> By being there, by doing exactly what you say, by being exactly who you are. It just takes time for people to see the consistency; there is no quick way to do that . . . When a young man got killed, his mother didn't have enough money to bury him, so our Bible class raised $1,000 and gave it to her. And we didn't put any pressure on her to come to our church, because we love her . . . See, everybody is accustomed to doing things with strings attached, they aren't accustomed to things happening when there are no strings.

At Tree of Life, members are motivated by an explicit common ethical system, and one that emphasizes charity, love, and sense of duty to others. These explicit values not only encourage trust among members, but make trusting safe, pleasurable, and rational.[10]

The members of Tree of Life have also granted their community the moral authority to have expectations of their responsibilities. In this case, such moral authority originates in religious or doctrinal beliefs, as a matter of faith. In other cases, such authority can arise from feelings of belonging to, and being jointly responsible for, the community that claims one as a member. Belonging comes from sharing a set of foundational values with other members of the community, and trust is built as people act as their community expects of them.

When people invest themselves in the voluntary associations that constitute the immediate social context of their lives, they help to create the first line of social trust. Becoming connected as an individual aggregates to powerful forces of moral authority. Because they are "spontaneous" institutions, "intermediate communities distinct from the family or those deliberately established by governments," such associations are the product of accumulated social trust, and emblematic of individuals' feelings of connections to institutions beyond the family.[11]

THE CHALLENGE OF CARING IN PUBLIC

Despite the value of shared social trust, for many of us, connections to public sources of moral authority are tenuous and fragile. There are any number of reasons why it is harder to care "in public" than within the private sphere of family and friends. Some of these have to do with the nature of care itself: caring emphasizes belonging, and belonging can easily turn to exclusion. Caring requires trust, but racial, ethnic, or class differences can be barriers to trust and prohibit the expression of caring. Other challenges are as much perceptual—relating to how we think about care—as structural. These challenges relate to such issues as what we think appropriate concerns for public life, who among us are caregivers and how caring should be shown, and the relative value of care versus other of life's pleasures.

One of the essentials of caring is the creation in the one cared for of feelings of security and safety. Programs that care for youths go to great lengths to make young people feel part of a group and to regard themselves and their peers as part of a familylike structure. As one Block Brother explained:

> That's what I focus on in my group, making that family bond . . . it doesn't matter what you have . . . as long as you're all together, stay together, look out for each other . . . I have the older ones look after the younger ones, even if they not related . . . 'cause when they in my group, they related, you know? No matter what, now all of them have that friendship and that bond that they gonna have no matter what, regardless if I'm there or not. And when they go off to school they know, "oh yeah, that guy's in my block brother group, he's a friend of mine."

But caring for young people is also about teaching them to care. What do young people learn when group belonging is stressed? How can this important mechanism of caring be reconciled to an ethic that suggests that one should care for outsiders just as one cares for members of one's group? Does a focus on within-group care diminish the authenticity of caring? Are there circumstances in which such divisions might be warranted?

The larger question is whether a focus on groups and belonging supports or facilitates discrimination against outsiders. Even if our formal groupings strive to avoid exclusion on terms of race, gender, class, or religion, does the process of building up a feeling of group belonging send a message that discrimination in more informal settings is acceptable? How does it affect our habits of interaction with people different from us?

An individual's "map" of caring activities was described in the previous section as a series of concentric circles emanating from self to family, friends, and other members of an individual's social groups. It is all too easy to describe this schema of caring as a natural construction of enlightened self-interest, and to deduce from this observation a vision of care as a mechanism for sustaining the reciprocal supports of a group. If care is viewed solely as an means of social exchange, then it is not too difficult to argue for restricting one's caring efforts to exclusive groups; and from there to justify groups that benefit insiders at the expense of others.

Research on youth gangs, for example, has documented that a great deal of caring goes on within gang organizations.[12] Relationships built within these organizations can provide young people with material support, emotional security, and personal attention. Their membership and structure offer a sense of belonging. Yet gangs are certainly not caring for the outsiders on whom they prey. Can an organization that cares for its members while neglecting or even harming others be considered caring in any sense?

Other organizations, such as fraternities, are valued in part by their members for being exclusive or, at least, making strong distinctions between insiders and outsiders. Are such divisions inherently problematic, or do they represent opportunities for caring? The Alpha-Omega Boys Club in San Francisco, an organization that serves lower-income African American youths, has created a fraternity for some of the young men who associate there. The Club argues that this association represents a positive use of social discrimination by allowing its members an environment where their differences from the majority culture are celebrated and supported. Similar arguments have been made for separate associations of women, minorities, and disadvantaged groups in a broad range of contexts. Groups can be powerful supporting structures, and exclusive associations might be particularly important for individuals who need to gather and share their resources for growth and development. Building a sense of belonging and in-group care can be a valid strategy for building individual capacity and self-esteem.

Yet wherever belonging and group support are stressed, a conscious effort must be made to internalize values of equality, commonality, and acceptance as well. Young people need intentional guidance in creating a moral cosmos that resonates beyond their self-interest. An essential part of modeling care is demonstrating how circumstances and willful commitments can create connections beyond the social map of one's life. Life can be led with permeable boundaries of caring such that circles of care do not have to be organized solely around kin, ethnic groups, or social class. One can consciously work to create interlocking circles of care in which care relationships built around willful commitments coexist with those that arise more naturally and instrumentally.

Reaching out is also difficult because the caring process relies on trust between both parties to a care relationship, and trust is usually more difficult to build when ethnic or class differences separate us. It is harder to care for those who greet one's outreach with suspicion or indifference, and so one can fall into a habit of responding to those whose familiarity makes trusting less difficult. Understanding these barriers can fortify youths to work to overcome them. An appreciation of diverse cultures as well as an internalized sense of our fundamental similarities can help caregivers respond appropriately and genuinely. Part of teaching "willful commitment," therefore, is teaching strategies for attentiveness, responsiveness, and competence in caring for those whose perspectives might be very different from one's own.

Organized care providers can promote the development and reality of their members' moral cosmos in several ways. First, as we have seen, most caring organizations manage themselves thoughtfully and with great intentionality, attempting to model the values of caring in every facet of their operation. Taking on commitments beyond a natural or convenient sphere—such as adopting a family or church in another community, or engaging in social action on behalf of nonmembers—models principled commitments to those who participate. Organized care providers that straddle several communities can work to make theirs a place where connections across social groups are institutionally supported. At El Puente, for example, much of the social action work has focused on bringing the many ethnic groups in the area— Latinos, Hasidic Jews, Poles, and African Americans—together to organize around common concerns and reduce neighborhood tensions. Organizations serving more homogeneous communities can make efforts to be accessible and welcoming to outsiders and minorities, thereby both modeling acceptance and increasing opportunities to build relationships that arise from these new connections.

The perceptual challenges to caring in public are in many ways more difficult to address, since they reflect deep-rooted attitudes and values in mainstream American society. Many of the challenges to caring come from the way we structure our lives in modern times. As the philosopher Alisdair MacIntyre explains,

> modernity partitions each human life into a variety of segments, each with its own norms and modes of behavior. So work is divided from leisure, private life from public, the corporate from the personal. So both childhood and old age have been wrenched away from the rest of human life and made over into distinct realms. And all these separations have been achieved so that it is the distinctiveness of each and not the unity of the life of the individual who passes through those parts in terms of which we are taught to think and to feel.[13]

As our social relations are increasingly experienced as the adoption of a number of segmented roles—parent, friend, worker, and citizen—our relations with others are more likely to be unidimensional, focused on the particular context in which they occur, and fragmented from other aspects of our lives. In the process of segmenting our lives, in separating our roles as parents, as workers, and as members of a larger community, we have also segmented our notions of care. We are now more and more likely to delimit the relevant sphere of caring to a small portion of our lives. Care has been relegated to the "private" sphere, which more and more often means the context of personal relationships. The habits of interaction that characterize care have been made to seem appropriate only to our private lives. As care has been privatized, it has been made irrelevant in the public sphere. Care no longer has a voice in discussions of how we act as citizens and workers, or what we expect of our peers and leaders.

As care has been confined to the family, it has also become more exclusively a feminine activity. Caring for children is still primarily a woman's activity in most families, and the sphere of home more disproportionately under the mother's influence. When care happens only at home, it becomes defined only in terms of the maternal nurturing that characterizes it in that setting, and identified with feminine activities.[14] In her influential book, *The Reproduction of Mothering*, psychoanalyst Nancy Chodorow describes how the "feminization of care" is a self-reinforcing process. "Girls and boys expect and assume women's unique capacities for sacrifice, caring, and mothering." [15] As a girl identifies with her mother and internalizes her attitudes, she prepares herself for a caring role in the future. As boys reject their mothers in order to identify with masculine role models, however, they also reject the values of caring that have been so closely identified with her. Studies of nurturing behavior in young children have found no difference in nurturing behavior in children younger than five. Among older children, however, gender differences become more marked, with older girls showing more interest in babies than younger girls, and older boys less interest than younger boys. [16]

Mothers have been primary caregivers of young children for much of civilization, and there are probably good biological reasons for this. But boys do not have to be socialized away from care, and the model for care does not have to be so insistently maternal. Caregiving can take place in any number of community activities in which men might participate. We can care for each other and important issues and organizations in associations beyond the family. Moreover, both women and men have important roles to play in nurturing the young both at home and beyond. Separating private life so distinctly from the public and limiting caring's role solely to the private sphere has polarized caring along gender lines.

Not surprisingly, in being privatized and feminized, care has been devalued in the public sphere. The social status and presumed authority of teachers, youth workers, and others in the caring professions have diminished even as the demands of their jobs increase. The work of parenting has been reduced from a socially acceptable full-time effort to another household chore. Employers require overtime and demand productivity increases without having to ask what such demands do to the caregiving responsibilities of their workforce. Since so much of the caregiving that we do is for young people, devaluing care devalues youth as well.

In small details and in large choices, the message that care does not matter in public life trickles down to those we most want to protect from it, our children. To understand why care has been devalued in modern society, we must look carefully at the attitudes and assumptions that undergird our culture. Cultural values are expressed not only in rituals and special events, but in the structure and organization of everyday life. The mundane interactions of everyday life, the structure of our most ordinary institutions, the ways in which we treat children, young people, and the aged all contain deep metaphors about our fundamental beliefs about human nature and our purpose in life. When we think about culture we must examine these deep structures, not contenting ourselves with a review of the messages on the surface. [17]

One of the most striking developments in mainstream American society is the way in which pop psychology's language of self-actualization, personal fulfillment, and meeting of needs has been incorporated into ways of understanding commitment, obligation, responsibility, and "goodness."[18] The self-focused culture rests on the notion that there is no higher value than self-fulfillment, and that the self is the relevant unit for decision making. Self-help books that tout the discovery of and focus on personal desires, that teach us how to reduce stress, inhibition, and "co-dependence," glorify freedom from responsibility on any terms unpleasurable to us. These attitudes have even influenced the way caregivers view their efforts. In his study of caring in American life, *Acts of Compassion*, the sociologist Robert Wuthnow examined the ways in which the language used to describe care has changed in recent years. He found that the language of sacrifice, of *should*, was less apparent in his subjects' talk of care than in earlier accounts; in its place was talk of personal fulfillment and growth.[19]

Self-focused attitudes, or the rush to what some philosophers have called "radical freedom,"[20] are reinforced by consumerism, free-market economics, and the rationality that has led us to seek control over nature, the physical world, and all circumstances of human existence. We can see these attitudes at work in the organizing principles of schools, our major socializing institutions. Traditional educational psychology uses rewards and punishments and the confinement of classrooms, hierarchy, and fixed-grade progression to shape youths into instructable, achievement-oriented workers. Group work is encouraged in early years, but individual grades and achievements are what matters. While American schooling has been characterized by an endless array of reform efforts, few have attempted to change the "syntax of schooling," as one historian describes it, and none have succeeded.[21]

From these cultural attitudes, institutionalized in schooling, economic structure, and the media, young people are presented with the notion of a vast "system" over which one has little control and in the context of which one's appropriate response is to maximize one's individual status and personal fulfillment. Across the economic spectrum, the message is the same: the point is to get ahead, achieve for yourself, and don't extend yourself on behalf of others. "What they hear on the streets and in school is, you've gotta protect your own; don't worry about nobody else," said a Kansas City Block Brother. The preferred means of individual achievement may vary, but the ends are fairly similar: material success and protection from being "used" by others.[22] "The message at New Trier [High School] is you're nobody if you don't get good grades and go to a good college," said one young woman at The Warming House in suburban Chicago. A young facilitator at El Puente described the options young people see for "getting over on the system" in a poor community in Brooklyn:

> It's two really extreme points from which to look at the same problem . . . the young people look at their peers, those that . . . [are involved in] drug dealing or alternative methods of employment as semi-heros, as people that "got over" on the system . . . they're living comfortably and it's visible . . . and at the same time they're looking at the political aspects of the neighborhood and seeing the same thing . . . in the sense that . . .it's about how many votes can you get me the next time out. . . Either you get over on the system and you take the risk of getting caught and going to jail—or the other side which is power, influence, knowing so and so and they'll hook me up, that kind of deal. And in the middle, it looks like there's not much . . .

Part of the struggle, then, is demonstrating that there *is* something in the middle: that there is an alternative to a worldview organized around self and competition. It is about explaining life as inherently more complex and more hopeful than a faceless system. It is teaching that while there are inevitable conflicts between our own self-focused needs and between our needs and those of other people, it is by actively attempting to resolve them that growth and fulfillment occur. It is modeling a life built partially on natural affections and completed and sustained by "willed fidelities"—promises, covenants, and assumed responsibilities—and "intended acts of care."[23] It is picturing a world in which care is a public virtue, applicable to public endeavors, such as raising a generation, as well as to family. It is leading a life with limits and boundaries not unlike those established by the caring youth workers at Smokey House, Block Brothers, and The Warming House. As the young people who appreciate those limits understand, it is in a world of demands and expectations that one's best self emerges. Such a vision can be a "moral source" that can give both young people and those that care for them a source of energy, productivity, and meaning.

Caring is not just a topical ointment; it cannot merely be applied atop an unquestioned and unchanged system. It is in this respect that caring is subversive. A culture of care rests on values of mutuality, interdependence, and sharing burdens, values that challenge many of the assumptions that undergird our existing institutions. It challenges the notion that free-market economics, the primacy of individual rights, and Western notions of the self are in all cases appropriate means of constructing action in the world. It suggests a value system that views giving and getting not in terms of exchange mechanisms but as responses to others' needs. A culture of care recognizes caring, mutual help, and nurturance as explicitly public virtues, not domestic values imported into the public sphere. A culture of care asserts that *inter*dependence, not independence, is the desired outcome of healthy development and, by extension, the norm of social relations.

CHAPTER 8

REINVENTING CARE IN PUBLIC LIFE

As we reflect on the role of caring in young people's lives, what becomes clear is that youths need to grow up in a world infused with and organized by care. Although isolated encounters and refuges can be helpful, what really matters is consistent, coherent values that are lived, not just preached, in as many parts of their lives as possible. It is good, but not enough, to have a caring teacher; what a young person really needs is to attend a school where the values and practices of that teacher are celebrated, supported, and reflected in the actions of other adults, in the policies of the school, and in the eyes of the parents, community, and other institutions. To become the caring citizens we need them to be, young people need to have made real the vision of the interdependent life organized around public, as well as private, caregiving responsibilities. They must see the adults whom they admire devote themselves to willed fidelities and intentional caring, beyond self-focused achievements and pleasures. They must see care made the serious work of public life, rather than a private lifestyle choice. They must grow up in a true community, where they can both expect the constancy and trust of caring and know that such responsibility will be expected of them.

We must work to create a society where caring is a social norm. We must strive to become part of a real community, where each of us accepts responsibility for active participation in efforts to sustain our common values and promote the development of the next generation. We are a nation of associators, of neighbors. We have come together in the past to protect what we love and to fight for what we believe in. We can do so again, but to mobilize ourselves for this task we must reflect, discuss, and begin to distill what we really want and believe. We must individually and collectively choose caring—or trust, love, or any other moral source—as an organizing principle in our lives, and then together figure out what we must do to transform our world to reflect it.

CARE AS A SOCIAL NORM

Building a society in which caring is normative behavior—not the exception—demands the same kinds of efforts and attitudes that the caring organizations and communities portrayed in this book have taken on. It involves creating, on a large scale, the culture of care that so many organizations refer to as their most important quality. Caring organizations recognize that creating a climate of trust and care requires leaders to devote a great deal of effort and time to the task and to support others' investment in its creation as well. They understand that a caring atmosphere demands that values of trust and care be consistently encoded in actions as well as explicitly articulated. And they have made sustaining this atmosphere a stated goal of their management practices.

Developing these norms in society involves undertaking these practices both in large policy actions and in gestures of individual commitment. It is caring writ large in public attention and effort, as well as in face-to-face encounters. It is, first of all, a public commitment to pay attention to caring, to celebrate it, and to recognize it as a valued outcome. It means accepting the promotion of caring—rigorously defined—as a valid goal and fundable activity. It involves celebrating the efforts of those who have made caring their life's work, including teachers, youth workers, and others in caring professions. These are all activities that can be undertaken on an individual level, but also institutionalized in social policies and cultural practices.

Building norms of caring on a large scale also involves making public the values that characterize caring atmospheres: respect, mutual support, and generosity. It means applying what have recently been thought of as purely private norms of conduct to public actions and roles. It means judging public policy, as well as the public actions of individuals, according to these same standards. Similarly, we can use the components of caring practice as benchmarks for considering whether our communities and society are as caring as we'd like them to be. Just as the quality of care provided by an individual or characterizing an organization can be evaluated by its practices of attentiveness, responsiveness, and competence, so too we can ask whether a society is caring according to the same criteria.

But changing social norms is not only about changing values. Caring cannot be contracted out: if there is not enough care for youth, we must all become caregivers. Care is a practice, and in the most basic sense, caring in public requires that we care actively, and not just care about, the things we value. It is not enough that we want for all youths what we want for our own children; we must then work actively and collectively to see that young people are provided with what they need. We must attempt to practice the attentiveness, responsiveness, and competence that characterize personal acts of care in our public lives as well.

We know what young people need: they need to be enveloped in a context in which several adults know them well and will look out for them and support them as they grow. Such relationships are the central necessary resource for adolescents. Our task, then, is to determine what resources are necessary to make these relationships available to young people and then mobilize ourselves to deliver them. Since organized care settings appear to be a rich source of these relationships, we should avail ourselves of their potential and support, encourage, and contribute to their work. All of us might not be able to care directly for a young person. But we can care for and nurture those who do through both active efforts and ongoing consensus that their work is valuable.

In adopting care as a social norm, we are legitimizing its practice and acknowledging to others that it is a valued and worthwhile endeavor. Shifting attitudes, however gradually, can open up a space for others to care more openly and to speak of caring values as public priorities. It can help others find the courage to question whether the predominant values of independence, self-fulfillment, and competition are appropriate standards by which to organize all aspects of their lives. And it can set an example for our youths that their instincts toward cooperation, mutuality, and trust are well founded.

Thinking of caring as the expectation, not the exception, is the first step in developing our own habits of caring. As we come to see caring attitudes and behaviors as the rule, we naturally become more attentive to opportunities to care in our own lives. We are more "in practice," more habituated to caring actions. Just as we have gradually, over the course of a generation, become more aware of our responsibility to protect the environment—and developed habits, such as recycling and conserving resources, to express this value—so too we can come to adopt caring behaviors as habits that arise from our culturally based expectations of how people are supposed to behave toward each other.

But as with changing most behaviors, changing our attitudes toward caring will take a certain amount of "willed commitment." We will need, first of all, to accept limitations to our freedom and individualism that arise from considering the needs of both our loved ones and our fellow citizens. We will need to see the requirement that each individual's freedom is tempered by his or her responsibility to act on behalf of others as a good, a moral source for a more interdependent, caring society. Such a requirement is a departure from prevailing attitudes in mainstream culture, where talk is of one's right to do as he wishes so long as it causes no harm to another. In place of talk of rights, we will need to talk more extensively about our responsibilities to each other.[1]

Another important willed commitment is for each of us to make a conscious effort to create and act upon a moral cosmos that brings us beyond care for intimate others and friends to those for whom we might not naturally, or habitually, care. We need to find time and energy in our lives to bridge the divides between age, ethnicity, and social class that have occurred as people have focused on their natural circles of care. Caring for those outside our group is often more awkward, as cultural differences create barriers to trust and connection. Because the circumstances of such care are often more difficult, creating and sustaining such care relationships requires greater will and constant effort. Many of us will need to seek out opportunities for caring, extending ourselves first by learning awareness of the range of needs just outside our immediate circle. For others, the challenge will be to focus and commit oneself to the pressing needs at hand.

OPPORTUNITIES FOR CARING

We are a nation of associators. Alexis de Toqueville first noted this fact in 1831, in his book *Democracy in America*; and scholars since have explored the causes and consequences of American predilections for joining. De Toqueville and others have seen in our appetite for associations the roots of our economic prosperity and political stability. The sociologist Max Weber argued that the Puritan values of our nation's first immigrants instilled a national character that valued public trust and common effort.[2] The historian Francis Fukuyama describes the period of greatest economic growth in the United States as a time when Americans were relatively united around a moral language that stressed honesty, reliability, cooperativeness, and a sense of duty to others. Fukuyama explains that even during periods of large-scale immigration, mainstream American culture still cohered around shared values that emphasized the need to at times subordinate private interests to the larger goals of the community.[3]

Even today, despite claims of declining social involvement,[4] we are still a nation of volunteers and donors. A 1996 Gallup poll found that more than 93 million adults volunteered their time in 1995, almost half of the adult population. One quarter of those who volunteered contributed five hours or more of their time per week. More than two-thirds of all households reported that they had given money to charity in 1995; while the number of households contributing has declined in the last decade, the real dollar amount of contributions has increased.[5] The nonprofit sector in the United States is by far larger and more established than that in any other country in the world, including the developed countries of Western Europe and Japan.[6]

Volunteering in the service of youth development is a major part of charitable involvement in the United States. Approximately 15 percent of all adults volunteer their time to youth development activities; a similar number donated their time to educational institutions of all kinds. Approximately 20 percent of those that contribute to charity donated money to youth development programs in 1995, but contributions to youth development organizations are a very small fraction (less than 5 percent) of total contributions to charity.[7]

But a large "caring sector" does not necessarily imply a caring society.[8] While the United States has the largest nonprofit sector of any developed country, it also has the lowest level of public social welfare expenditures, and the disparity between U.S. government spending and that of other developed countries is not made up by private giving. In many of these countries, the government is regarded as the primary agent of caring. In the United States, on the other hand, recent polls suggest that fewer and fewer people believe that their government has the responsibility to care for people who cannot care for themselves.[9]

Although the voluntary sector can make a tremendous contribution to care for children, the elderly, and others in need, there is danger in romanticizing the potential of volunteers to address large-scale social needs. Many leaders of nonprofit organizations have expressed concern that recent cuts in social welfare spending have been advanced by some politicians on the grounds that voluntary, nongovernmental entities will be able to assume responsibility for those in need.[10] Their fear is that relying on the nonprofit sector might become an excuse for disregarding serious social and economic problems, and a barrier to a general acceptance on the part of all for responsibility for care of all of our fellow citizens.[11] It is evident that as those in need grow farther and farther away from us, they are harder for us to care for directly. The question is whether we continue to hold ourselves responsible to them.

Indeed, our patterns of giving and volunteering suggest that we must be wary of rhetoric that urges communities to "take care of their own." It is estimated that 85 to 90 percent of charitable donations are raised and spent locally.[12] Since the amount and targeting of giving varies significantly by income (as well as by other social and demographic indicators), the communities most in need are least able to generate private funds and volunteer time.

Volunteering in the service of one's own community is essential; for most, it is the first and most intense level of public involvement. There is much to be done in our own backyards. But if our aim is a caring society, it is not enough to cultivate our own gardens. We must find ways of widening our moral cosmos to include those who are usually out of view. It is important that we do this as individuals, that we take the time to reflect on our attentiveness to those outside our immediate circles and consider ways of reaching them. This is the work of building one's personal moral cosmos.

It is just as important that we widen the moral cosmos of the organizations of which we are a part. It is not enough for us to take action as individuals; we must also look to collective action and to the power and potential of all public institutions. We exist not as a mass of independent individuals, but rather in the context of a vast web of relationships; and these connections are what allow us to pursue collective action effectively.[13] Our efforts have meaning not only in our private roles as individuals, but in our capacities as community members, congregants, workers, and citizens. It is in these roles that we have opportunities to help reshape the moral cosmos of all kinds of institutions. We can encourage our church to reach out to a community with fewer resources. We can lobby our employer to establish and staff a mentoring program. We can help our child's school establish a service learning program that brings young people in contact with others of different ethnicity or social class. Every sector has a role to play in a caring society, whether by supporting, facilitating, or directly providing care to youths and those in need. Many different types of organizations can serve as agents of change; and we, in our capacities as members of these organizations, can help to marshal them to the cause of caring.

As we work to transform public institutions, we cannot fail to challenge assumptions about the role of government in caring. "New Federalism," block grants, and welfare reform have gradually unwound the social safety net in which federal government agencies directly provided care or material assistance to those in need. Most of the current debate has placed "government bureaucracy" squarely at odds with "personal initiative." But it is important to distinguish between government as a supporter, facilitator, and funder of care and government as a direct provider of care. We can, on the one hand, reject the notion of increasing government's role in direct caregiving and on the other advocate a widened role for public support of caring activities. We can see government in the service of a collective moral cosmos: government as an efficient means of helping us care for a wider circle of individuals than we personally, or the mediating institutions to which we belong, might be able to reach.

With respect to care for young people, few would probably argue for a government-issued mentor for each youth. But government funds could be available to support local mentoring initiatives that seek to move beyond their communities. Public funds could support youth service programs, like Vista and Americorps, that are locally directed and staffed. More public dollars could support the recreation, arts, and other youth development programs where youth workers build relationships with young people. Members of the workforce temporarily or permanently displaced from their occupations could be retrained and redeployed in caring professions. These examples do not imply the creation of a vast new bureaucracy to care for youth. They are basically more of the same; but on a much larger scale. What they do imply, however, is a collective public will to make care for youth a priority, and to devote the resources necessary to make it a reality.

Speaking of a collective moral cosmos presumes that we have one. We do. There lies in most of us enough common notions of the value of democracy, the inherent dignity of each individual, and our fundamental equality as human beings that we can find a moral source to guide us in the decisions we face. But these ideals are buried and, for the most part, unspoken. We are desperately in need of public dialogue about our values and our common goals. It is only with consensus on these issues that we as a country will be able to generate priorities and make the difficult choices required to effect them. And it is only by having the courage to confront the decisions required to create caring public policy that we will ever be able to stop reacting to the effects of lack of care, and begin to act to help provide it.

This is democracy in process. It involves taking responsibility for choices and priorities as citizens, rather than abdicating to experts and politicians both the practice of care and the setting of priorities around it. It requires public debate that surfaces "our concerns and the values they reflect . . . the consequences for what we value of the different courses of action open to us . . . the hard choices between conflicting values that would enable us to establish priorities; and hence . . . a general direction or range of action that all of us could go along with, thereby permitting our elected officials to devise solutions that will prove both effective and sustainable because they are widely supported."[14]

In short, the first step each of us must take to caring citizenship is to take responsibility. We must each take responsibility not only for an individual child or even for a whole generation, but for the entire meaning of care itself. We must each join in the dialogue.

BEGINNING THE JOURNEY

The philosopher and educator Paolo Friere has described dialogue as "the encounter of men addressed to the common task of learning and acting."[15] and it is in this spirit that we must begin our individual and collective journeys toward caring in public. Using caring as an organizing principle, we can reflect on how we as individuals, how the organizations of which we are a part, and how the community and nation in which we live meet our expectations of care for future generations.

Our dialogue will also need to be informed by more, and better, research. We need more research that follows individuals throughout their lives to understand continuity and the effects of intervention; that focuses on the many complex factors that interact to affect development; that identifies the specific behaviors that demonstrate caring. We need research on the process of care, as well as its outcomes. And we need to know more about the possibilities and limitations of intentional, organized care.

What follows are questions that might be useful in spurring individual and group reflection as well as research. While not an exhaustive list, this set of questions refers to the many aspects of care that have been discussed in earlier chapters. They are meant to offer examples of how the themes of this book can be used in an exercise of self- and group evaluation.

- How do we practice attentiveness in our private and public relations? To whom are we responsive, and what are the boundaries of our responsiveness? What caring competencies do we possess, and which would we like to develop? What skills or capacities would make us more effective caregivers?
- What are our culturally based assumptions about the practice of care? What do we see as appropriate boundaries for the content and intimacy of our caring practices for our own children and for those in our charge? What do we assume about the motivations of others and their "natural instincts?" What do we know about the expectations and assumptions of others from different ethnic or social groups?
- How are the young people in our care asked to take responsibility for the care relationship? What evidence of mutuality do we expect? How do our youth tend to show it? What expectations do we have for their behavior toward us and toward each other?
- How well do we distinguish between competent, responsible caregiving and irresponsible or exploitive practices? How well have we taught our children and those in our care to identify appropriate settings for them-

selves? What characteristics do we believe are most important to this distinction?

- How do we manage the constraints on our ability to care for youth? What are the practical limits to our involvement? What are the boundaries on our relationships with any individual young person? How do we make them understood? What are our expectations of our efforts?

- What is our ideal image of a caring youth (or a caring person)? How do we promote an ethic of care among our own children and those in our care? What messages do we convey to youths about their responsibilities to others and to their environments? How consistent are these messages across the life of our children or a young person in our care?

- What opportunities do our youths have to demonstrate and practice care? Are there expectations of caring practices at home, at school, and in other contexts? What role models do they have for caring behaviors and values?

- What outcomes do we think we are affecting in caring for youths? To what outcomes are we held responsible by others? How important is it that we demonstrate caring's value in quantifiable terms? What we would choose as indicators of our success?

- What messages do the decision-making practices, groupings, and norms of interaction in our family/our organization/our society send to young people? How do these messages promote caring or instill cynicism about caring values? How consistent are our explicit messages and those implicit in our actions? How do we demonstrate that caring "pays?" How intentionally do we model care, and what other opportunities for modeling exist?

- How do the activities in which we engage our children and those in our care promote or discourage caring? In what other ways might we encourage them in caring practices?

- How effectively do we create an atmosphere of caring in our family/our organization/our community? What strategies and practices might help us encourage this spirit? By what practices do we demonstrate support for young people and those that care for them?

- How do we make our family/our organization/our community a safe and trusted place for youths? How accessible are we to the young people in our care and to each other? How do we show young people that they are listened to?

- How well are we making connections across the family, school, and community contexts of the lives of our children and those in our care? What are we doing to foster relationships among all those involved in a young person's life? How are we supporting others who care for the young person?

- What are the "moral sources" that organize our lives? What does our "moral cosmos" look like, and how does it compare to the natural circles of care for family, friends, and members of our community? How much responsiveness do we show to concerns in our moral cosmos? How might we support the development and reality of our own and our children's moral cosmos?
- What is the level of trust in our family/our organization/our community/our society? What expectations can members hold of each other? What responsibilities do members accept, and why? How might trust be enhanced? How much trust exists between our group and others? What are the barriers to trust both within our group and across groups? What are we doing to reach across the divides that separate groups?
- In what parts of our lives do we practice and expect care? Are we supporting and expecting the same levels of caring behavior in young men as we do in young women? What models of caring behavior are we offering young people?
- What values do the priorities and actions of our everyday lives model for our children and those in our care? How are we demonstrating a life of willed fidelities and intended acts of care? How do we show that mutuality, interdependence, and community are useful and rewarding values?

For better or worse, it is impossible for us to begin a journey of reflection on our care for youth and not end up questioning our own values and the way we are living our lives. The messages and values we wish to convey, the climate of trust and safety we wish to create, and the behaviors and habits we wish to encourage are all the product of the care we practice in our own lives. Caring for youths in isolation of these contexts is a deprived and artificial form of care. If we are serious about providing more care to youths and helping them to become caring, involved citizens, we cannot merely create enclaves of caring in their lives. We must do whatever possible to make caring values the pervading atmosphere of their whole lives.

This is not to suggest that we should despair if we cannot influence the entire context of our children's lives or those of the youths in our care. We must have realistic expectations. The attitudes and pressures that hinder caring—the culture of radical individualism, a worldview that sees all social interaction as exchanges based on self-interest—arise from deep-seated values and beliefs. The key is for us not to give up: not to assume that competition and self-focused pursuits are "just human nature"; not to worry that our youths will fail if they are taught to question prevailing attitudes about success and self-preservation; not to fear to trust or teach our children to fear it.

Here, then, is how caring can be truly subversive: we can begin to chip away, one block at a time, at the barriers to caring in our own lives and in the organizations and communities of which we are a part. Through small actions and sustained, willed commitments, we can begin, ever so gradually, to question the norms and attitudes that are taken for granted in our culture, and open up a space for others to do the same. By approaching our relationships with our own children and those in our care with a new intentionality, we can help the next generation become more caring and community-minded than our own. By supporting the community-based, "mediating institutions" that provide much of the organized care for youth, we can strengthen the foundations and connections of a healthy social network both for our families and for those whom we might not know. And by actively working to practice care in a moral cosmos that includes those who are different from us, we can begin to reach across the divides that threaten our country's unity and moral purpose.

These are small, isolated actions but, if performed with a vision of a caring culture, they can constitute a revolution. Finding words to describe our vision is the first step: once we have a common goal in mind, we can reach it one step at a time. This is a grand conspiracy in which each of us can play a role. Join the revolution.

1. Caring for Our Youth: A Call to Action

1. Paolo Freire, *Pedagogy of the Oppressed*, trans. Myra Bergman Ramos (New York: Seabury Press, 1970), p. 76.

2. The Block Brothers program was phased out of current Kansas City Boys and Girls offerings in 1999 as a new facility in the targeted community was brought into operation. Current management believe that they cannot afford to support both the Block Brothers program and the facility, but expect to initiate the Block Brothers program in other communities of Kansas City in need of programs and services for youth.

3. Freire, *Pedagogy of the Oppressed*, p. 78.

4. Peter L. Berger and Richard John Neuhaus, *To Empower People: The Role of Mediating Structures in Public Policy* (Washington, D.C.: American Enterprise Institute, 1977).

5. While such "markers of a caring society" do not yet exist, cross-national indicators of child well-being, for use in informing international child policy making and planning, are currently being developed by an international group of organizations representing twenty nations. This group has focused on six topics: census and survey data, primary research, administrative data, children's rights, policy perspectives, and childhood as a stage in itself. In addition, the participants are exploring how these topics areas are related to five domains of children's lives: social connectedness, civic life skills, personal life skills, safety and physical status, and children's activities. The results of this project will be an important first step toward understanding the social, physical, and economic conditions under which children

and youths survive globally. Asher Ben-Arieh and Helmut Wintersberger, eds., *Monitoring and Measuring the State of Children—Beyond Survival* (Vienna: European Centre for Social Welfare Policy and Research, 1997).

6. Sudhir Alladi Venkatesh, "Learnin' the Trade: Conversations with a Gangsta,'" *Public Culture* 6 (1994): 319–41; Venkatesh, "The Killing of Rail: Black Gangs and the Reconstruction of 'Community' in an Urban Ghetto" (Chicago: Center for the Study of Urban Inequality, University of Chicago).

2. The Practice of Care

1. This model of the caring process draws upon the work of H. Richard Niebuhr, Joan Tronto, and Bernice Fisher and Joan Tronto, among others. See especially Joan Tronto, *Moral Boundaries: A Political Argument for an Ethic of Care* (New York: Routledge, 1993); H. Richard Niebuhr, *The Responsible Self: An Essay in Christian Moral Philosophy* (San Francisco: Harper and Row, 1963); and Bernice Fisher and Joan Tronto, "Toward a Feminist Theory of Care," in Emily Abel and Margaret Nelson, eds., *Circles of Care: Work and Identity in Women's Lives* (Albany: State University of New York Press, 1991). Although their influences on my thought are profound, the model presented, and especially its flaws, is my responsibility alone. In citing these philosophers I do not mean to imply that they have accepted or are even aware of the thoughts presented here.

2. Nel Noddings, *Caring: A Feminine Approach to Ethics and Moral Education* (Berkeley: University of California Press, 1984), p. 14.

3. Carol Gilligan, *In a Different Voice: Psychological Theory and Women's Development* (Cambridge: Harvard University Press, 1982); and Gilligan et al., *Mapping the Moral Domain: A Contribution of Women's Thinking to Psychological Theory and Education* (Cambridge: Harvard University Press, 1988).

4. William M. Sullivan, "Philosophical and Definitional Issues Related to Caring," Paper commissioned by the Lilly Endowment Research and Grants Program on Youth and Caring, 1992, p. 25.

5. Alasdair MacIntyre, *A Short History of Ethics* (New York: Macmillan, 1996).

6. Tronto, *Moral Boundaries*, p. 6 and ch. 2.

7. Hobbes, as quoted in MacIntyre, *A Short History of Ethics*, p. 132.

8. Sigmund Freud, *Civilization and Its Discontents*, trans. James Strachey (New York: Norton, 1961), p. 59.

9. R. Trivers, "The Evolution of Reciprocal Altruism," *Quarterly Review of Biology* (1971): 35–37.

10. Hazel Markus and Shinobu Kitayama, "Culture and the Self: Implications

for Cognition, Emotion, and Motivation," *Psychological Review* 98 (1991): 224–53; cited in Barry Schwartz, "Why Altruism Is Impossible . . . and Ubiquitous, *Social Science Review* (1993): 314–43). See also Richard Shweder, *Thinking Through Cultures: Expeditions in Cultural Psychology* (Cambridge: Harvard University Press, 1991).

11. Philippe Aries, *Centuries of Childhood: A Social History of Family Life*, trans. Robert Baldick (New York: Knopf, 1962), p. 128; and Joseph Kett, *Rites of Passage: Adolescence in America, 1790 to the Present* (New York: Basic Books, 1977), p. 112.

12. Kett, *Rites of Passage*; also Kenneth Kenniston, *Youth and Dissent: The Rise of a New Opposition* (New York: Harcourt, Brace, Jovanovich, 1971) on the emergence of youth as a time of life.

13. Thomas Weisner and Ronald Gallimore, "My Brother's Keeper: Child and Sibling Caretaking," *Current Anthropology* 18 (June 1977): 169–90.

14. See, especially, Harold Cheatham and James Stewart, eds., *Black Families: Interdisciplinary Perspectives* (New Brunswick, N.J.: Transaction Publishers, 1990).

15. Patricia Hill Collins, "Black Women and Motherhood," in Virginia Held, ed., *Justice and Care: Essential Readings in Feminist Ethics* (Boulder: Westview Press, 1995).

16. See Diana Baumrind, "The Influence of Parenting Style on Adolescent Competence and Substance Use," *Journal of Early Adolescence* 11, no. 1 (1991): 56–95; Baumrind, "Rejoinder to Lewis' Reinterpretation of Parental Firm Control Effects: Are Authoritative Families Really More Harmonious?" *Psychological Bulletin* 94 (1983): 132–42; and also Collins, "Black Women and Motherhood."

17. Charles Hayes, Alice Ryan, and Elaine Zseller, "Middle School Child's Perceptions of Caring Teachers," *American Journal of Education* 103 (1994): 1–19.

18. Kris Bosworth et al., "Phase I: Describing Caring Institutions and Individuals, September 1, 1992–July 31, 1994." Final Report to the Lilly Endowment (Bloomington, Ind.: Center for Adolescent Studies, School of Education, Indiana University, 1994).

19. Daniel Coyle, *Hardball: A Season in the Projects* (New York: Putnam, 1993); and Carol Stack, *All Our Kin: Strategies for Survival in a Black Community* (New York: Harper and Row, 1974).

3. Mutuality, Trust, and Boundaries

1. See Jeffery Fisher, Arie Nadler, and Bella DePaulo, eds., *New Directions in Helping*, vol. 1: *Recipient Reactions to Aid* (New York: Academic Press for research on the determinants of how care is received, 1983.

2. Nel Noddings, *Caring: A Feminine Approach to Ethics and Moral Education* (Berkeley: University of California Press, 1984).

3. See Fred Hechinger, *Fateful Choices: Healthy Youth for the 21st Century* (New York: Hill and Wang, 1992), ch. 7; George Noblit, "Power and Caring," *American Educational Research Journal* 30, no. 1 (1992): 23–38; Robert Slavin, *Cooperative Learning: Theory, Research, and Practice* (2nd ed.; Boston: Allyn and Bacon, 1994); and John McKnight, *The Careless Society: Community and Its Counterfeits* (New York: Basic Books, 1995) for more discussion of this issue.

4. Samuel P. Oliner and Pearl M. Oliner, *The Altruistic Personality: Rescuers of Jews in Nazi Europe* (New York: Free Press, 1988), p. 249.

5. Oliner and Oliner, *The Altruistic Personality*, p. 160.

6. Eric Erikson, *Childhood and Society* (New York: Norton, 1963); Erikson, *Identity: Youth and Crisis* (New York: Norton, 1968); and Erikson, *The Life Cycle Completed: A Review* (New York: Norton, 1982).

7. See J. Bowlby, *A Secure Base: Parent-Child Attachment and Healthy Human Development* (New York: Basic Books, 1988); M. D. S. Ainsworth, M. C. Blehar, E. Waters, and S. Wall, *Patterns of Attachment* (Hillsdale, N.J.: Lawrence Erlbaum Associates, 1978); R. R. Kobak and A. Sceery, "Attachment in Late Adolescence: Working Models, Affect Regulation, and Representations of Self and Others," *Child Development* 59 (1988): 135–46; R. Emde, "The Wonder of Our Complex Enterprise: Steps Enabled by Attachment and the Effects of Relationships on Relationships," *Infant Mental Health Journal* 12 (1991): 164–73; L. A. Stroufe, "The Role of Infant-Caregiver Attachment in Development," in J. Belsky and T. Nezwoksi, eds., *Clinical Implications of Attachment* (Hillsdale, N.J.: Lawrence Erlbaum Associates, 1988); and L. A. Stroufe and J. Fleeson, "Attachment and the Construction of Relationships," in Willard Hartup and Zick Rubin, eds., *Relationships and Development* (Hillsdale, N.J.: Lawrence Erlbaum Associates, 1986) for further discussion of attachment theory.

8. Eisenberg, *The Caring Child*, pp. 41–43.

9. Milton Mayeroff, *On Caring* (New York: Harper and Row, 1971), p. 38.

10. Paul Edwards, *Buber and Buberism: A Critical Evaluation* (Lawrence: Department of Philosophy, University of Kansas, 1971).

11. Noddings, *Caring*, pp. 8, 83.

12. Martin Buber, as quoted in Paul Edwards, *Buber and Buberism*, p. 21.

13. Robert Wuthnow, *Acts of Compassion: Caring for Other and Helping Ourselves* (Princeton: Princeton University Press, 1991), ch. 7.

14. Although the Block Brothers program was phased out of current Kansas City Boys and Girls offerings in 1999, current management expects to initiate the Block Brothers program in other communities of Kansas City in need of programs and services for youth.

4. Learning to Care

1. William M. Sullivan, "Philosophical and Definitional Issues Related to Caring," Paper commissioned by the Lilly Endowment Research and Grants Program on Youth and Caring, 1992.

2. Samuel P. Oliner and Pearl M. Oliner, *The Altruistic Personality: Rescuers of Jews in Nazi Europe* (New York: Free Press, 1988), p. 249.

3. Oliner and Oliner, *The Altruistic Personality*, p. 160.

4. P. Linsday Chase-Lansdale, Lauren Wakschlag, and Jeanne Brooks-Gunn, "A Psychological Perspective on the Development of Caring in Children and Youth: The Role of the Family," Paper commissioned by the Lilly Endowment Research Grants Program on Youth and Caring, 1992.

5. Beatrice B. Whiting and John W. M. Whiting, *Children of Six Cultures: A Psycho-Cultural Analysis.* Cambridge: Harvard University Press, 1975; also Michael Schulman and Eva Mekler, *Bringing Up a Moral Child: A New Approach for Teaching Your Child to Be Kind, Just, and Responsible* (Reading, Mass.: Addison-Wesley, 1985).

6. See for example, Paul Mussen and Nancy Eisenberg-Berg, *Caring, Sharing, and Helping: The Roots of Prosocial Behavior in Children* (San Francisco: W. H. Freeman, 1977); Nancy Eisenberg and Paul Mussen, *The Roots of Prosocial Behavior in Children* (Cambridge: Cambridge University Press, 1989); Nancy Eisenberg, *The Caring Child* (Cambridge: Harvard University Press, 1992); M. E. Lamb, "Sibling Relationships Across the Lifespan," in M. E. Lamb and B. Sutton-Smith, eds, *Sibling Relationships* (Hillsdale, N.J.: Lawrence Erlbaum Associates, 1982); and J. Dunn and P. Munn, "Siblings and the Development of Prosocial Behaviors, *International Journal of Behavioral Development* 9(1986): 265–84.

7. Lawrence Kohlberg, *Essays in Moral Development* (San Francisco: Harper and Row, 1981); Jean Piaget, *The Moral Development of the Child* (Glencoe, Ill.: Free Press, 1948); Nancy Eisenberg, Paul Miller, Rita Shell, Sandra McNalley, and Cindy Shea, "Prosocial Development in Adolescence: A Longitudinal Study," *Developmental Psychology* 27, no. 5 (1991): 849–57; and Martin Hoffman, "The Contribution of Empathy to Justice and Moral Judgement," in Bill Puka, ed., *Moral Development*, vol. 7: *Reaching Out: Caring, Altruism, and Prosocial Development* (New York: Garland, 1994).

8. S. Seymour, "Cooperation and Competition: Some Issues and Problems in Cross-Cultural Analysis," in Ruth H. Munroe, Robert L. Munroe, and Beatrice B. Whiting, eds., *Handbook of Cross-Cultural Human Development* (New York: Garland STPM Press, 1981).

9. The Whitings' research is summarized in a series of books, the most relevant of which to this essay are Beatrice B. Whiting and John W. M. Whiting, *Children of*

Six Cultures: A Psycho-Cultural Analysis (Cambridge: Harvard University Press, 1975); and Beatrice B. Whiting and Carolyn Pope Edwards, *Children of Different Worlds: The Formation of Social Behavior* (Cambridge,: Harvard University Press, 1988).

10. Whiting and Whiting, *Children of Six Cultures*, p. 71.

11. In the 1960s Masden and his colleagues developed a series of games that have been used with rural and urban children in the United States, Israel, Korea, and several other countries, and with aboriginal and Caucasian children in Canada, Australia, New Guinea, and New Zealand. One such game, the "cooperation board," is a square with four circles and four strings controlling a single pen. Four children each take hold of a string such that no one child can control the pen without others' cooperation. When told that the group would be rewarded for drawing a line through all four circles, children of all cultures were able to cooperate; but when children were told that they would receive individual rewards for drawing a line through their own circle, children from rural and aboriginal subcultures continued to cooperate, while children from more "complex" cultures began to compete in a nonadaptive manner, sometimes so ferociously that their strings would break or the board would topple. Moreover, children in cultural transition—aboriginal children educated in Caucasian schools, or first-generation immigrants from rural areas—demonstrated that they were slowly acquiring the competitive habits of the modern societies to which they were exposed. See L. Mann, "Cross-cultural Studies of Small Groups," in H. Triandis and R. Brislin, eds., *Handbook of Cross-Cultural Psychology*, vol. 5: *Social Psychology* (Boston: Allyn and Bacon, 1980), for a review of the research conducted using the Madsen procedures.

12. Seymour, "Cooperation and Competition"; H. D. Fishbein, *The Psychology of Infancy and Childhood: Evolutionary and Cross-Cultural Perspectives* (Hillsdale, N.J.: Lawrence Erlbaum Associates, 1984); also Margaret Mead. *Cooperation and Competition Among Primitive Peoples* (Boston: Beacon Press, 1967).

13. Whiting and Edwards, *Children of Different Worlds*, p. 159.

14. C. Ember, "Feminine Task Assignment and the Social Behavior of Boys," *Ethos* 1(1973): 424–39.

15. Whiting and Whiting, *Children of Six Cultures*.

16. Oliner and Oliner, *The Altruistic Personality*, pp. 165–66.

17. M. Csikszentmihalyi, "Intrinsic Rewards and Emergent Motivation," in M. R. Lepper and D. Greene, eds., *The Hidden Costs of Reward* (Hillsdale, N.J.: Lawrence Erlbaum Associates, 1978); and Eisenberg, *The Caring Child*, p. 95.

18. Eisenberg, *The Caring Child*, pp. 93–94.

19. E. Midlarsky. Competence and helping: Notes toward a model. In Staub, et.al. *The Development and Maintenance of Prosocial Behavior*, 291-308.

20. R. Coles, *The Moral Life of Children* (Boston: Atlantic Monthly Press, 1986), p. 28.

21. Gordon Parker, Elaine Barrett, and Ian Hickie, "From Nurture to Network: Examining Links Between Perceptions of Parenting Received in Childhood and Social Bonds in Adulthood," *American Journal of Psychiatry* 149, no. 7 (1992): 877–85.

22. Suanne Ostendorf, "A Study of the Relationship Between Women's Perceptions of How They Were Parented and Their Development of Intimate Relationships," Ph.D. dissertation, West Virginia University, 1991.

23. Emmy E. Werner and Ruth S. Smith, *Vulnerable But Invincible: A Longitudinal Study of Resilient Children and Youth* (St. Louis: McGraw-Hill, 1982); Gina O'Connell Higgins, *Resilient Adults: Overcoming a Cruel Past* (San Francisco: Jossey-Bass, 1994); and Parker, Barret, and Hickie, "From Nurture to Network."

24. Emmy E. Werner and Ruth S. Smith, *Overcoming the Odds: High Risk Children from Birth to Adulthood* (Ithaca: Cornell University Press, 1992).

25. Werner and Smith, *Overcoming the Odds*, p. 138.

26. Werner and Smith, *Overcoming the Odds*; see also G. H. Elder, (1986). Military times and turning points in men's lives. *Developmental Psychology* 22, no. 2 (1986): 233–45; and J. V. Long and G. E. Vaillant, "Natural History of Male Psychological Health, XI: Escape from the Underclass," *American Journal of Psychiatry* 141 (1984): 341–46. In light of these studies, it is interesting to note that current entry requirements into the military include not only a high school diploma, but some college credit as well.

27. David W. Proefrock, "Adolescence: Social fact and Psychological Concept," *Adolescence* 16, no. 64(1981): 851–58.

28. Robert M. Gallatzer-Levy and Bertram J. Cohler. (1993). *The Essential Other: A Developmental Psychology of the Self.* New York: Basic Books.

29. See Ernest S. Wolf, John E. Gedo, and David M. Terman, "On the Adolescent Process as a Transformation of the Self," *Journal of Youth and Adolescence* 1, no. 3(1972): 257–72; and Wolf, "Adolescence: Psychology of the Self and Selfobjects," *Adolescent Psychiatry* 10(1982): 171–81, for more discussion of this view.

30. See, for example, W. W. Hartup and S. G. Moore, "Early Peer Relations: Developmental Significance and Prognostic Implications," *Early Childhood Research Quarterly* 5(1990): 1-17; Laurence Steinberg, "Latchkey Children and Susceptibility to Peer Pressure: An Ecological Analysis," *Developmental Psychology* 22, no. 4(1986): 433–39.

31. Daniel Hart, *Inner-City Youth Committed to Care: The Contributions of Self-Understanding, Parents, and Teachers.* Report to the Lilly Endowment Research Grants Program on Youth and Caring, 1990; Daniel Hart and Suzanne Fegley, "Altruism and Caring in Adolescence: Relations to Self-Understanding and Social

Judgement," Paper supported by the Lilly Endowment Research and Grants Program on Youth and Caring, 1994.

32. Werner and Smith, *Overcoming the Odds*, 199.

33. Ibid.

34. Several major studies underway may provide more robust evidence of service learning's impact on youth. These include: "Learn and Serve America K-12," a project funded by the Corporation for National and Community Service, which is being evaluated by the Center for Human Resources at Brandeis University and Abt Associates, Inc.; "CalServe" (California's Learn and Serve America's Programs), which is being evaluated by RPP International through a grant from California's Department of Education; "Research Study of the Impact of Exemplary Service Learning Programs on Achievement," part of a larger study, funded by the Kellogg Foundation, entitled the "National Service Learning Initiative;" "Active Citizenship Today (ACT)," which is operated by the Close-Up Foundation and Constitutional Rights Foundation, and funded principally by the DeWitt Wallace-Reader's Digest Fund; and the "Service Learning Impact Study," examining the impact of the Helper Model of Service Learning. See *Proceedings from the Service Learning Summit, September 9-10, 1995* (Minneapolis: Search Institute, 1996) for more information about these studies.

35. Hecht, Schine, and their colleagues have developed measures to assess changes in the feelings and potential actions of young people who participate in service experiences. One measure they have developed involves gauging adolescents' responses to a series of scenarios reflecting typical interpersonal problems encountered in service environments. See Deborah Hecht, Dana Fusco, Joan Schine, and Nancy Berkson, "Assessing Caring in Young Adolescent Students Participating in Service Learning," Paper presented at the annual meeting of the American Psychological Association, New York, 1995; Joan Schine, "Measuring Caring: A Report to the Lilly Endowment." Final report to the Lilly Endowment Research Grants Program on Youth and Caring, 1991; and Joan Schine, "Young Adolescents and Community Service," Carnegie Council on Adolescent Development Working Paper (Washington, D.C.: Carnegie Council on Adolescent Development, 1989).

36. Hecht, Fusco, Schine, and Berkson, "Assessing Caring in Young Adolescent Students."

37. Thomas H. Batchelder and Susan Root, "Effects of an Undergraduate Program to Integrate Academic Learning and Service: Cognitive, Prosocial Cognitive, and Identity Outcomes," *Journal of Adolescence* 17, no. 4 (1994): 341–55.

38. L. O'Donnell, A. Steuve, A. San Dolval, and R. Atnafou, "Violence Prevention and Young Adolescents' Participation in Community Youth Service," *Journal of Adolescent Health* 24 no. 1 (1999): 28–37.

39. Brian O'Connell. "Long-Term Effects of School-Community Service Projects," Ph.D. dissertation, State University of New York, Buffalo, 1983.

40. Schine, "Young Adolescents and Community Service"; Howe, "Can Schools Teach Values?" Remarks at Lehigh University, 1986; and Presidents' Science Advisory Committee, *Youth: Transition to Adulthood* (Washington, D.C.: GPO, 1973). See also cross-cultural research by Whiting and Whiting.

41. A 1981 review of school-sponsored experiential learning programs, including 10 community service programs, found gains in social and personal responsibility measures among community service participants that were not found in control groups. Another study of several community service programs found that participants gained a greater sense of responsibility to the community outside of school. A study of high school seniors engaged in both required and voluntary community service projects found no changes, compared to nonparticipants, in attitudes toward social or personal responsibility. However, students whose service commitments were more extensive showed meaningful changes in attitude. College students participating in a for-credit community service program showed a significant increase in their belief that people can make a difference and in their own commitment to community service. A study of adolescent volunteers involved in community improvement and child care projects in New York State found that participants' attitudes toward social responsibility changed, but found no change in participants' sense of personal duty to meet others' needs. Similarly, a study of a youth service program in which young adolescents were paired with senior citizens in nursing homes found no change in the participants' attitudes toward the elderly over the course of the program. A study of the psychological effects of a required community service class in high school found no changes in quantitative measures of social interest, helping disposition, or other measures, although qualitative measures did show changes.

See Dan Conrad and Diane Hedin, *Executive Summary of the Final Report of the Experiential Education Evaluation Project* (St Paul: University of Minnesota, Center for Youth Development and Research, 1985); Fred M. Newmann and Robert A. Rutter, *The Effects of High School Community Service Programs on Students' Social Development* (Madison: University of Wisconsin, Wisconsin Center for Education Research, 1983); Robert M. Williams, *The Effects of Required Community Service on the Process of Developing Responsibility in Suburban Youth* (Lincoln: University of Nebraska, 1993); Dwight E. Giles and Janet Eyler, "The Impact of a College Community Service Laboratory on Students' Personal, Social, and Cognitive Outcomes," *Journal of Adolescence* 17, no. 4 (1994):327–39; Stephen F. Hamilton and Mickey L. Fenzel, "The Impact of Volunteer Experience on Adolescent Social Development: Evidence of Program Effects," *Journal of Adolescent Research* 3, no. 1 (1988): 65–80; Kenneth Maton, "Meaningful Involvement in Instrumental Activity and Well-Being: Studies of Older Adolescence and At-Risk Teen-Agers," *American*

Journal of Community Psychology 18, no. 2 (1990): 297–320; Kenneth Maton, James X. Bembry, and Alfred de la Cuesta, "Youth and Caring Activity and Positive Youth Development: Creating Environments Where Youth Can Care." Final report to the Lilly Endowment Research Grants Program on Youth and Caring, n.d.; Eric Bradley Middleton, "The Psychological and Social Effects of Community Service Tasks on Adolescents," Ph.D. dissertation, Purdue University, 1993; and Frances McConnell Williams, "Re-Engineering a Movement—Reclaiming Youth at Risk: An Assessment of Selected Outcomes of Community Service Learning Experiences in an Urban High School," Ph.D. dissertation, University of Illinois, Urbana-Champaign, 1997.

42. Robert A. Rutter and Fred M. Newmann, "The Potential of Community Service to Enhance Civic Responsibility," *Social Education* 53, no. 6 (1989): 371–74; but Judy Reese, "The Impact of School-Based Community Services on Ninth-Grade Students' Self-Esteem and Sense of Civic Inclusion," Ph.D. dissertation, Rutgers University, 1997, did find that students who participated in community service programs scored higher on tests of civic inclusion than those who had not performed community service.

43. Kathleen Parks Luchs, "Selected Changes in Urban High School Students after Participation in Community Based Learning and Service Activities," Ph.D. dissertation, University of Maryland, 1981; Stephen F. Hamilton and Mickey L. Fenzel, "The Impact of Volunteer Experience on Adolescent Social Development: Evidence of Program Effects," *Journal of Adolescent Research* 3, no. 1 (1988): 65–80; Kenneth Maton, "Meaningful Involvement in Instrumental Activity and Well-Being"; James Leonard Krug, "Select Changes in High School Students' Self-Esteem and Attitudes Toward Their School and Community by Their Participation in Service Learning Activities at a Rocky Mountain High School," Ph.D. dissertation, University of Colorado, Boulder, 1993. In a 1982–83 study of high school youths involved in community service, volunteers expressed a greater sense of competence in working on collective tasks and in dealing with adults than did nonvolunteers. A study of the effects of participation in community service on adolescents with disabilities found that moderately and profoundly disabled adolescents, in particular, improved their self-images through service in which they were able to give assistance to others. See Fred M. Newmann and Robert A. Rutter, *The Effects of High School Community Service Programs on Students' Social Development* (Madison: University of Wisconsin, Wisconsin Center for Education Research, 1983); and Cathy Brill, "The Effects of Participation in Service-Learning on Adolescents with Disabilities," *Journal of Adolescence* 17, no. 4 (1994): 369–80.

44. An examination of the effects of a community-based learning and service experience on urban high school students found that students involved in the

program demonstrated positive and significant gains in responsibility for others, in competence to act upon the feeling of concern for others, and in their beliefs that they could make a difference. See Luchs, "Selected Changes in Urban High School Students After Participation in Community Based Learning and Service Activities."

45. Rutter and Newman, "Potential of Community Service to Enhance Civic Responsibility."

46. Hamilton and Fenzel, "Impact of Volunteer Experience on Adolescent Social Development."

47. Robert Wuthnow, *Learning to Care: Elementary Kindness in an Age of Indifference* (New York: Oxford University Press, 1995); Dan Conrad and Diane Hedin. (1989). *High School Community Service: A Review of Research and Programs.* St. Paul: University of Minnesota, National Center on Effective Secondary Schools, 1989.

48. Maton, "Meaningful Involvement in Instrumental Activity and Well-Being."

49. R. Shumer, "Community-Based Learning: Humanizing Education, *Journal of Adolescence* 17, no. 4 (1994): 357–67; Luchs, "Selected Changes in Urban High School Students After Participation in Community Based Learning and Service Activities." Maton and his colleagues, however, found significant reduction in absences in only one of two sites studied, and only over the long term. Maton, Bembry, and de la Cuesta, "Youth and Caring Activity and Positive Youth Development."

50. Brill, "Effects of Participation in Service-Learning on Adolescents with Disabilities"; G. E. Switzer, R. G. Simmons, M. A. Dew, J. M. Regalski, and C. Wang, "The Effect of a School-Based Helper Program on Adolescent Self-Image, Attitudes, and Behavior," Paper presented at the biannual meeting of the Society for Research on Adolescence, San Diego, 1994; R. L. Calabrese and H. Schumer, "The Effects of Service Activities on Adolescent Alienation, *Adolescence* 21 (1996): 675–87.

51. Diane Hedin, "Students as Teachers: A Tool for Improving School Climate and Productivity," *Social Policy* 17 (1987): 42–47.

52. G. B. Markus, J. Howard, and D. C. King, "Integrating Community Service and Classroom Instruction Enhances Learning: Results from an Experiment," *Educational Evaluation and Policy Analysis* 15 (1993): 410–19; K. E. Dewsbury-White, "The Relationship of Service Learning Project Models to the Subject Matter Achievement of Middle School Students," Ph.D. dissertation, Michigan State University, 1993; S. F. Hamilton and R. S. Zeldin, "Learning Civics in the Community, *Curriculum Inquiry* 17 (1987): 407–20.

53. Studies of experiential learning have shown that community service, as well as other experience-based learning programs, can improve students' problem-solving abilities relative to comparison groups that do not participate in such programs. A study of undergraduates involved in service learning courses found that

participants showed significant growth in cognitive dimensions such as awareness of multidimensionality. Dan Conrad and Diane Hedin, "The Impact of Experiential Education on Adolescent Development," in Conrad and Hedin, eds., *Child and Youth Services, Special Issue, Youth Participation and Experiential Education* 4 (1982): 57–76; however, Schollenberger found no correlation between the amount of time spent in service learning programs and higher levels of thinking. J. W. Schollenberger, "Opportunities for Higher Levels of Thinking as They Occur in Service Learning," Ph.D. dissertation, University of Michigan, 1985.

54. A study of seventh graders randomly assigned to a school "helper program" in which participation in some type of helping activity was required throughout the school year found no effects on attitudes toward school relative to a control group. Similarly, a study of a science tutoring project for minority seventh grade students found no changes in attitudes toward learning among most participants. However, a study of the Community-Based Learning program, a dropout prevention effort sponsored by the Job Training Partnership Act, found that youth service can be a catalyst for improved attitudes toward school, particularly if the experience connects youths with adults and college students in the community. Switzer et al., "Effects of a School-Based Helper Program"; L. Dean and S. W. Murdock, "The Effect of Voluntary Service on Adolescent Attitudes Toward Learning," *Journal of Volunteer Administration* (1992): 5-10; and Schumer, "Community-Based Learning."

55. See especially Wuthnow, *Learning to Care*.

5. But What Does Caring "Accomplish"?

1. The idea of assets working in concert is more fully explored in the Search Institute's Healthy Development for Youth work; see Nancy Leffert, Peter Benson, and Jolene Roehlkepartain, *Starting Out Right: Developmental Assets for Children* (Minneapolis: Search Institute, 1997).

2. Leffert, Benson, and Roehlkepartain, *Starting Out Right*.

3. J. H. House, K. R. Landis, and D. Umberson, "Social Relationships and Health," in Peter Conrad and Rochelle Kern, eds., *The Sociology of Health and Illness: A Critical Perspective* (New York: St. Martin's Press, 1994).

4. Sheldon Cohen and S. Leonard Syme, "The Study and Application of Social Support," in Cohen and Syme, eds., *Social Support and Health* (Orlando: Academic Press, 1985).

5. T. A. Wills, "Supportive Functions of Interpersonal Relationships," in Cohen and Symes, eds., *Social Support and Health*.

6. J. B. Jemmott and S. E. Locke, "Psychosocial Factors, Immunologic Media-

tion, and Human Susceptibility to Infectious Diseases: How Much Do We Know? *Psychological Bulletin* 95 (1984): 78—108.

7. R. W. Blum and P. M. Rinehart, *Reducing the Risk: Connections that Make a Difference in the Lives of Youth*, Preliminary report of the National Longitudinal Study of Adolescent Health, Division of General Pediatrics and Adolescent Health, University of Minnesota, 1997; Cynthia Fink, "A Study of the Relationship of Perceived Social Support and the Components of Self-Care Agency in Adolescents," Ph.D. dissertation, University of North Carolina College of Nursing, Charlotte, 1988; Kathleen Fox Tennant, "The Relationship Among Self-Esteem, Social Support, and Health Behaviors Among Adolescents," Ph.D. dissertation, Ohio University, 1993

8. See Emmy E. Werner, Jessie M. Bierman, and Fern E. French, *The Children of Kauai* (Honolulu: University of Hawaii Press, 1971); Emmy E. Werner and Ruth S. Smith. *Kauai's Children Come of Age* (Honolulu: University of Hawaii Press, 1977); Werner and Smith, *Vulnerable but Invincible: A Longitudinal Study Resilient Children and Youth* (St. Louis: McGraw-Hill, 1982, 1989); and Werner and Smith, *Overcoming the Odds: High Risk Children from Birth to Adulthood* (Ithaca: Cornell University Press, 1992) for complete review of the results of this study.

9. Emmy E. Werner, "The Role of Caring Adults and Religious Coping Efforts in the Lives of Children of Alcoholics," Final report to the Lilly Endowment Research Grants Program on Youth and Caring, n.d.

10. M. D. Resnick, L. J. Harris, and R. W. Blum, "The Impact of Caring and Connectedness on Adolescent Health and Well-Being," *Journal of Pediatric Child Health* 29, no. 1 (1993): s3–s9.

11. For perspectives on the influence of social context in cognitive development, see L. S. Vygotsky, *Mind in Society: The Development of Higher Psychological Processes* (Cambridge: Harvard University Press, 1978); also Barbara Rogoff, *Apprenticeship in Thinking: Cognitive Development in Social Context* (New York: Oxford University Press, 1990). Other developmentalists concerned with the socially situated nature of cognition include Jean Lave and Etienne Wegner, *Situated Learning: Legitimate Peripheral Participation* (New York: Cambridge University Press, 1991); and Lauren B. Resnick, John M. Levine, and Stephanie D. Teasley, *Perspectives on Socially Shared Cognition* (Washington, D.C.: American Psychological Association, 1991).

12. J. Finn, "Withdrawing from School,," *Review of Education Research* 59 (1989): 117–42.

13. Carol Goodenow, "Classroom Belonging Among Early Adolescent Students: Relationships to Motivation and Achievement," *Journal of Early Adolescence* 13 (1993): 21–43.

14. E. A. Skinner, J. G. Wellborn, and J. P. Connell, "What It Takes to Do Well in School and Whether I've Got It: The Role of Perceived Control in Children's Engagement and School Achievement," *Journal of Educational Psychology* 82: (1990): 22–32.

15. Skinner and Belmont, "Motivation in the Classroom."

16. R. Ryan, J. Stiller, and J. Lynch. "Representations of Relationships to Teachers, Parents, and Friends as Predictors of Academic Motivation and Self-Esteem," *Journal of Early Adolescence* 14 1994: 226–49.

17. C. Midgley, H. Feldlaufer, and J. S. Eccles, "Student/Teacher Relations and Attitudes Toward Mathematics Before and After the Transition to Junior High School," *Child Development* 90 (1989): 981–92; Midgley, Feldlaufer, and Eccles, "The Transition to Junior High School: Beliefs of Pre- and Post-Transition Teachers." *Journal of Youth and Adolescence* 17 (1988): 543–62.

18. Pung-Kil Lee, "A Case Study: Students' Perceptions of Caring Manners of Educational Leaders and Its Relation to Their Learning Outcomes," Ph.D. dissertation, Florida State University, 1993.

19. Joycelyn Gay Parish, "Student Perceptions of Teacher Caring and Student At-Risk Behaviors, Achievement, Attendance, and Behavior Toward Teachers," Ph.D. dissertation, Kansas State University, 1992.

20. E. A. Skinner and M. J. Belmont, "Motivation in the Classroom: Reciprocal Effects of Teacher Behavior and Student Engagement Across the School Year," *Journal of Educational Psychology* 85 (1993): 571–81.

21. Lee, "A Case Study."

22. Kris Bosworth, "Caring for Others and Being Cared For: Students Talk Caring in School," *Phi Delta Kappan* (1995): 686–93.

23. See, especially, Boomer, Lester, Onore, and Cook, *Negotiating the Curriculum* (London and Washington, D.C.: Falmer Press, 1992); and J. S. Thomases, "Challenging the Norms: Democracy, Empowering Education, and Negotiating the Curriculum," *New Designs for Youth Development* 14, no. 3: (1998): 30–35.

24. V. A. Lee and A. S. Bryk, "A Multilevel Model of the Social Distribution of High School Achievement," *Sociology of Education* 62: (1989): 172–92.

25. R. W. Roeser, C. Midgley, and M. L. Maehr, "Unfolding and Enfolding Youth: A Cross-Sectional Study of Perceived School Culture and Students' Psychological Well-Being," Paper presented at the Biennial Meeting of the Society for Research on Adolescence, San Diego, Calif., 1994

26. P. A. Haensly and J. L. Parons, "Creative, Intellectual, and Psychosocial Development Through Mentorship, *Youth and Society* 25, no. 2 (1993): 202–21.

27. J. P. Allen, B. J. Leadbeater, and J. L. Aber, "Adolescent Problem Behaviors: The Influence of Attachment and Autonomy," *Pediatric Clinics of North America* 37 (1990): 35–47. Quoted in J. E. Rhodes, J. M. Cotreras, and S. C. Mengelsdorf, "Nat-

ural Mentor Relationships Among Latina Adolescent Mothers: Psychological Adjustment, Moderating Processes, and the Role of Early Parental Acceptance," *American Journal of Community Psychology* 22, no. 2 (1994): 211–27.

28. See, for example, E. P. Torrance, *Mentor Relationships: How They Aid Creative Achievement, Endure, Change, and Die* (Buffalo, N.Y.: Bearly, 1984); D. J. Levinson, *The Seasons of a Man's Life* (New York: Alfred A. Knopf, 1978); and E. G. C. Collins and P. Scott, eds., "Everyone Who Makes It Has a Mentor," *Harvard Business Review* 56, no. 4 (1978): 89–101.

29. J. E. Rhodes, L. Ebert, and K. Fischer, "Natural Mentors: An Overlooked Resource in the Social Networks of African-American Adolescent Mothers," *American Journal of Community Psychology* 20 (1992): 445–62; Rhodes, Contreras, and Mangelsdorf, "Natural Mentor Relationships Among Latina Adolescent Mothers."

30. Elena Lee Klaw, "Natural Mentors in the Lives of African-American Pregnant and Parenting Adolescents," Ph.D. dissertation, University of Illinois, Urbana-Champaign, 1998.

31. An evaluation of a multi-site mentoring and advocacy program serving inner-city Baltimore youths from sixth through twelfth grades found that schools that had been successful in establishing a mentoring program as a part of their student support effort were more likely to show improvements in student attendance and report card grades. J. P. McPortland and S. M. Nettles, "Using Community Adults as Advocates or Mentors for At-Risk Middle School Students: A Two-Year Evaluation of Project RAISE, *American Journal of Education* 99, no. 4 (1991): 568–86. See also W. Robinson, "Mentoring as a Transition to Success: A Cross-Racial Model," Ph.D. dissertation, University of Wisconsin, Madison, 1997.

32. J. Lee and B. Cramond, "The Positive Effects of Mentoring Economically Disadvantaged Students," *Professional School Counseling* 2, no. 3 (1999): 172–81.

33. A. W. Johnson, "Mentoring At-Risk Youth: A Research Review and Evaluation of the Impact of the Sponsor-A-Scholar Program on Student Performance," Ph.D. dissertation, University of Pennsylvania, 1997.

34. Kristine V. Morrow and Melanie B. Styles, *Building Relationships with Youth in Program Settings: A Study of Big Brothers/Big Sisters* (Philadelphia: Public/Private Ventures, 1995).

35. Morrow and Styles, *Building Relationships with Youth*.

36. See especially the Parental Bonding Instrument, in G. Parker, "The Parental Bonding Instrument: Psychometric Properties Reviewed," *Psychiatric Development* 4 (1989): 317–35; the EMBU, in C. Perris, L. Jacobsson, H. Lindstrom, L. Von Knorring, and H. Oerris, "Development of a New Inventory for Assessing Memories of Parental Rearing Behavior," *Acta Psychiatrica Scandinavica* 61 (1980): 265–74; the Family Adaptability and Cohesion Evaluation Scales II, and the Parent-Adolescent

Communication Index, in D. H. Olson, H. I. McCubbin, H. Barnes, A. Larsen, M. Muxen, and M. Wilson, *Family Inventories: Inventories Used in a National Survey of Families Across the Life Cycle* (2nd rev.; St. Paul: Family Social Science, University of Minnesota, 1994); the Parental Behavior Measure, in G. W. Peterson, "Parental Behavior Measure," manuscript, University of Tennessee, Department of Child and Family Studies, Knoxville, 1982; and the Intimacy Scale, in D. A. Blyth and F. S. Foster-Clark, "Gender Differences in Perceived Intimacy with Different Members of Adolescents' Social Networks," *Sex Roles* 17 (1987): 689–719, for assessments of parental support. And see especially Boggs's Adolescent Social Support Inventory, in K. Boggs, "Pubertal Status and Social Support Seeking Behavior in Early Adolescents," *Journal of Pediatric Nursing* 3, no. 4 (1988): 229–35, for measures of social support.

37. In the school environment, perhaps the most widely used general measure is the Classroom Environment Scales, which cover a broad range of social issues within the classroom, including teacher support and student affiliation. Two newer questionnaires, the Psychological Sense of School Membership Scale and the Classroom Belonging and Support Scale, were developed by Carol Goodenow of Tufts University to gauge students' sense of belonging in their schools and their feelings of acceptance and support by teachers and classmates. See R. Moos and E. Trickett, *Classroom Environment Scale Manual* (Palo Alto, Calif.: Consulting Psychologists Press, 1974); and, more recently, C. Goodenow, "The Psychological Sense of School Membership Among Adolescents: Scale Development and Educational Correlates," *Psychology in the Schools* 30 (1993): 79–80; and C. Goodenow, "Conceptualizing and Measuring Classroom Belonging and Support Among Adolescents," Paper presented at the biennial meeting of the Society for Research in Adolescence, San Diego, Calif., 1994.

38. Joan Schine and her colleagues at the National Service Learning Center developed a multimethod approach to evaluating the caring competence of youths involved in the Early Adolescent Helper Program. Helpers' skills in showing others that they care was rated by their teachers and their peers, as well as by independent observers who watched the helpers interact with the children or senior citizens at their placement site. In addition, the helpers were individually interviewed about how they see themselves demonstrating care for others and were asked to respond to a series of scenarios designed to elicit their construction of caring behaviors.

Martin Ford, a psychologist at Stanford University, also developed a multimethod technique to evaluate the caring competence of adolescents. He developed a series of scenarios in which a competent, caring adolescent's help is required, and had students rate the degree to which they would be willing to help in the situation and the degree to which they would feel competent to help. In addition he had both students and teachers nominate those students in their classrooms whom they thought would be most competent and willing to help in each of the situations. Self-report and peer/teacher nominations complement each other: self-reports might be subject to self-enhancing response bias, whereas teachers and peers provide more reliable estimates of a subject's caring competence. On the other hand, teachers and peers tend to be relatively insensitive to contextual variations in students' caring competence, nominating the same students as likely to help in all situations, whereas in self-report measures students often indicate that they would be more willing and able to help in one situation than another. Thus, both types of measures provide useful information. See Joan Schine, "Measuring Caring: A Report to the Lilly Endowment," Final report to the Lilly Endowment Research Grants Program on Youth and Caring, 1991; and Martin Ford, "An Empirical Investigation of the Psychological Processes Underlying Caring Behavior Patterns in Adolescence," Final report to the Lilly Endowment Research Grants Program on Youth and Caring, 1995.

39. Michael Lewis, Candice Feiring, and Saul Rosenthal, "The Development of Caring." Final report to the Lilly Endowment Research Grants Program on Youth and Caring, 1995.

40. Saul Rosenthal and Michael Lewis, "Doing, Saying, and Thinking: Is There Coherency in Moral Behavior?" (New Brunswick, N.J.: Institute for the Study of Child Development, Robert Wood Johnson Medical School, n.d.).

41. Carolyn S. Henry, "Family Antecedents of Caring Behavior in Adolescents," Report to the Lilly Endowment Research Grants Program on Youth and Caring, 1995.

42. See, especially, the Interpersonal Reactivity Index, in M. H. Davis, "A Multidimensional Approach to Individual Differences in Empathy," *JSAS Catalog of Selected Documents in Psychology* 10 (1980): 85; the Questionnaire Measure of Emotional Empathy, in A. Mehrabian and N. Epstein, "A Measure of Emotional Empathy," *Journal of Personality* 40 (1972): 525–43; also N. Eisenberg, E. Cameron, and K. Tryon, "Prosocial Behavior in the Preschool Years: Methodological and Conceptual Issues," in E. Staub, D. Bartal, J. Marylowski, and J. Reykowski, eds., *The Development and Maintenance of Prosocial Behavior: Positive Morality* (New York: Plenum, 1984.

43. Dan Conrad and Diane Hedin, "Instruments and Scoring Guide of the Experiential Education Evaluation Project" (St. Paul: University of Minnesota, Center for Youth Development and Research, 1981).

44. See, for example, Robert M. Gallatzer-Levy and Bertram J. Cohler, *The Essential Other: A Developmental Psychology of the Self* (New York: Basic Books, 1993); Ernest Wolf, "On the Developmental Line of Selfobject Relations," in Arnold Goldberg, ed., *Advances in Self Psychology* (New York: International Universities

Press, 1980); Robert Putnam, *Making Democracy Work: Civic Traditions in Modern Italy* (Princeton: Princeton University Press, 1993); Putnam, "Bowling Alone: America's Declining Social Capital," *Current* 373 (1995); and Peter Berger and Richard Neuhaus, *To Empower People: The Role of Mediating Structures in Public Policy* (Washington, D.C.: American Enterprise Institute for Public Policy Research, 1977) for a discussion of both points of view.

6. Sustaining Care: Caring Schools and Other Organizations

1. Samuel B. Bachrach, "Caring Organizations: An Oxymoron?" Final report to the Lilly Endowment Research Grants Program on Youth and Caring, 1996.

2. See James P. Comer, *School Power: Implications of an Intervention Project* (New York: Free Press, 1980), and James Comer, Norris M. Haynes, and Muriel Hamilton-Lee, "School Power: A Model for Improving Black Student Achievement," in Will DeMarcell Smith and Eva Wells Chunn, eds., *Black Education: A Quest for Quality and Excellence* (New Brunswick, N.J.: Transaction Publishers, 1989) for a more thorough review of the Comer Schools philosophy and operation.

3. James Comer, "Building Quality Relationships, in Josie G. Bain and Joan L. Herman, eds., *Making Schools Work for Underachieving Minority Students: Next Steps for Research, Policy, and Practice* (New York: Greenwood Press. 1990).

4. V. Battistich, D. Solomon, D. Kim, M. Watson, and E. Schaps, "Schools as Communities, Poverty Levels of Student Populations, and Students' Attitudes, Motives, and Performance: A Multilevel Analysis," *American Educational Research Journal* 32 (1995): 627–58; V. Battistich, E. Schaps, M. Watson, and D. Solomon, "Prevention Effects of the Child Development Project: Early Findings from an Ongoing Multisite Demonstration Trial," *Journal of Adolescent Research* 11 (1996): 12–35. See also C. Lewis, E. Schaps, and M. Watson, "The Caring Classroom's Academic Edge, *Educational Leadership*, 1996.

5. See, for example, William Kahn, "Caring for the Caregivers: Patterns of Organizational Caregiving," *Administrative Science Quarterly* 38 (1993): 539–63; Wilmar Schaufeli, Christina Maslach, and Tadeusz Marek, eds., *Professional Burnout: Recent Developments in Theory and Research* (Washington, D.C.: Taylor and Francis, 1993; Christina Maslach, *Burnout: The Cost of Caring* (Englewood Cliffs, N.J.: Prentice-Hall, 1982; and Cary Cherniss, *Staff Burnout: Job Stress in the Human Services* (Beverly Hills: Sage, 1980.

6. See Bachrach, "Caring Organizations," for a more complete discussion of structures and practices to avoid burnout and support caring.

7. However, research has shown that parental influence is strongest in elemen-

tary school; the importance of parental involvement in high school has been less clearly demonstrated. Many researchers have found that parents tend to be far less involved in their children's high school experience, perhaps because they feel inadequately prepared to help with the subject material, because they do not feel welcome at school, or because they think their children do not need their help. However, an analysis of more than 28,000 high school seniors from the High School and Beyond longitudinal study found that parental involvement has a strong, positive effect on high school seniors' grades. Moreover, a newly published 10-year study of 20,000 high school students found that in the absence of parental engagement, young people are more influenced by a peer culture that demeans high academic performance and serves as a negative influence on attitudes toward school. Such evidence suggests that efforts to connect parents to their children's high school experience ought to be an essential component of school reform. For an overview of the literature on the effects of parental involvement across the school years, see T. V. Keith, "Parental Involvement and Achievement in High School." in Steven B. Silvern, ed., *Literacy Through Family, Community, and School Interaction* (Greenwich, Conn.: JAI Press, 1991); C. W. Hickman, G. Greenwood, and M. D. Miller, "High School Parent Involvement: Relationships with Achievement, Grade Level, SES, and Gender," *Journal of Research and Development in Education* 28, no. 3 (1995): 125–34; and Laurence Steinberg, *Beyond the Classroom: Why School Reform Has Failed and What Parents Need to Do* (New York: Simon and Schuster, 1996).

8. Joan Goodman, Virginia Sutton, and Ira Harkavy, "The Effectiveness of Family Workshops in Middle School Settings: Respect and Caring Make the Difference," in Robert J. Chaskin and Diana Mendley Rauner, eds., "A Kappan Special Section on Youth and Caring, *Phi Delta Kappan* 76, no. 9 (1995).

9. Steven Schinke and Roxanne Spillet, "The Effect of Boys and Girls Clubs on Promoting Caring in Public Housing," in Paul G. Shervish, Virginia A. Hodgkinson, Margaret Gates, and Associates, eds, *Care and Community in Modern Society: Passing On the Tradition of Service to Future Generations* (San Francisco: Jossey-Bass, 1995), pp. 177–87.

7. Building a Caring Community

1. Robert Wuthnow, *Acts of Compassion: Caring for Others and Helping Ourselves* (Princeton: Princeton University Press, 1991), p. 58.

2. Charles Taylor, *Sources of the Self: The Making of the Modern Identity* (Cambridge: Harvard University Press, 1989). I am grateful to William Sullivan, whose

paper, "Philosophical and Definitional Issues Related to Caring," led to Taylor's moral sources.

3. Care for the self is often overlooked in studies of care, perhaps because, having posited a relational viewpoint, it is difficult to extract individual selves from the relations in which they are formed. Care for the self is not selfishness, because it does not imply an inability or unwillingness to care for others. The contrast of care for the self to selflessness, on the other hand, can be illustrative. To care for oneself is to acknowledge that the self is worthy of the same attention that one focuses on others. It is a recognition of the necessity of considering one's own desires and needs while responding to those of others. With such consideration comes the responsibility to practice the same aspects of care for oneself—attending to one's situation and feelings, assessing one's needs, and responding to them—as one ideally performs for others. See Nel Noddings, *The Challenge to Care in Schools: An Alternative Approach to Education* (New York: Teachers College Press, 1992).

4. Nel Noddings, *Caring: A Feminine Approach to Ethics and Moral Education* (Berkeley: University of California Press, 1984).

5. Peter Berger and Richard John Neuhaus, *To Empower People: The Role of Mediating Structures in Public Policy* (Washington, D.C.: American Enterprise Institute, 1977), p. 2.

6. R. M. Kramer and T. R. Tyler, "Whither Trust?" in R. M. Kramer and T. R. Tyler, eds., *Trust in Organizations: Frontiers of Theory and Research* (Thousand Oaks, Calif.: Sage. 1996).

7. James S. Coleman, *Foundations of Social Theory* (Cambridge: Belknap Press of Harvard University Press, 1990).

8. Kramer and Tyler, "Whither Trust?'

9. I am indebted to R. M. Kramer, M. B. Brewer, and B. A. Hanna, "Collective Trust and Collective Action: The Decision to Trust as a Social Decision," in R. M. Kramer and T. R. Tyler, eds., *Trust in Organizations,* for previously summarizing these points.

10. From his cross-cultural analysis of the role of trust in economic prosperity among nation-states, the historian Francis Fukuyama argues that while all moral communities will create some degree of trust among their members, those that emphasize values of honesty, charity, cooperativeness, and sense of duty to others tend to be most successful in establishing trust among larger communities. Francis Fukuyama, *Trust: The Social Virtues and the Creation of Prosperity* (New York: Free Press, 1995).

11. Fukuyama, *Trust*, p. 27.

12. See, for example, Sudhir Alladi Venkatesh, "Learnin' the Trade: Conversations with a Gangsta," *Public Culture* 6 (1994): 319–41; and Venkatesh, *The Killing of*

Rail: Black Gangs and the Reconstitution of 'Community' in an Urban Ghetto (Chicago: Center for the Study of Urban Inequality, University of Chicago. n.d.).

13. Alasdair MacIntyre, *After Virtue: A Study in Moral Theory* (2nd ed.; Notre Dame, Ind.: University of Notre Dame Press, 1984), p. 202.

14. The notion of "benevolence" as a feminine virtue extends back to the Victorian era, when the distinctions between private and public life became most radically pronounced. See Rosemary Radford Ruether, "The Cult of True Womanhood," *Commonweal* 99, no. 6 (1973): 127–32, for an overview of this history.

15. Nancy Chodorow, *The Reproduction of Mothering: Psychoanalysis and the Sociology of Gender* (Berkeley: University of California Press, 1978), p. 83.

16. Phyllis Berman, "Young Children's Responses to Babies: Do They Foreshadow Differences Between Maternal and Paternal Styles?" in Alan Fogel and Gail F. Melson, eds., *The Origins of Nurturance: Developmental, Biological, and Culture Perspectives on Caregiving* (Hillsdale, N.J.: Lawrence Erlbaum, 1986).

17. It is perhaps for these reasons that many view the character education movement with some concern. Clearly, promoting caring values is a laudable end, but one must question whether attempting to teach these values in isolation can have much effect. Without examining the ways in which existing social, political, and economic structures (including that of the classroom!) offer conflicting messages, an effort to articulate and demonstrate values "on the surface" does nothing to address the assumptions that guide an individual's behavior. Such an effort runs the risk of promoting caring, and other moral values, as optional strategies for action in appropriate cases, rather than as a value system to undergird one's public and private behavior.

18. Don S. Browning, *Religious Thought and the Modern Psychologies* (Philadelphia: Fortress Press, 1987).

19. Wuthnow, *Acts of Compassion*, p. 115.

20. William M. Sullivan, "Philosophical and Definitional Issues Related to Caring," Paper commissioned by the Lilly Endowment Research and Grants Program on Youth and Caring, 1992.

21. David Tyack and Larry Cuban, *Tinkering Toward Utopia: A Century of Public School Reform* (Cambridge: Harvard University Press, 1995).

22. The urban anthropologist Elijah Anderson has described how the influence of the "old head" in inner-city communities has waned as the values of responsibility, restraint, and deferred gratification that these community leaders preach and embody have eroded. These ministers, policemen, or blue-collar workers who historically played an important role in socializing the youths of their community have lost their relevance for young people for whom these values have less meaning. Anderson argues that the teachings of the old head make little sense

to young men socialized to the prevailing values of the larger culture and facing few opportunities for legitimate employment in the inner cities. Elijah Anderson, *Streetwise: Race, Class, and Change in an Urban Community* (Chicago: University of Chicago Press, 1990), as quoted in Marc Freedman, *The Kindness of Strangers: Adult Mentors, Urban Youth, and the New Volunteerism* (San Francisco: Jossey-Bass, 1993).

23. Browning, *Religious Thought and Modern Psychologies*, p. 206.

8. Reinventing Care in Public Life

1. Amitai Etzioni, *The Spirit of Community: The Reinvention of American Society* (New York: Simon and Schuster, 1993).

2. Max Weber, *The Protestant Ethic and the Spirit of Capitalism*. Trans. Talcott Parsons. New York: Scribner, 1958

3. Francis Fukuyama. *Trust: The Social Virtues and the Creation of Prosperity* (New York: Free Press, 1995).

4. Robert Putnam. "Bowling Alone: America's Declining Social Capital," *Current* 373 (1995); John Clark, "Shifting Engagements: Lessons from the 'Bowling Alone' Debate," Husdon Briefing Paper, no. 196, 1996.

5. Independent Sector, *Giving and Volunteering in the United States: Findings from a National Survey* (Washington, D.C.: Independent Sector, 1996), p. 3.

6. Paul Schervish, Virginia Ann Hodgkinson, Margaret Jane Gates, and Associates, eds., *Care, Community, and Modern Society: Passing the Tradition of Service to Future Generations* (San Francisco: Jossey-Bass, 1995), p. 375..

7. Independent Sector, *Giving and Volunteering in the United States*.

8. Lester Salamon and Helmut Anheir, "Caring Sector or Caring Society: Discovering the Nonprofit Sector Cross-Nationally," in Schervish, Hodgkinson, Gates, and Associates, eds., *Care, Community and Modern Society*.

9. In 1988, 81.3% of respondents to Independent Sector's Gallup Poll on giving and volunteering agreed with the statement, "Government has responsibility to take care of people who can't take care of themselves." In 1996, 60.1% of respondents agreed with that statement, a decline of 25%. Independent Sector, *Giving and Volunteering in the United States*, pp. 3–82.

10. Gary Walker, *Can Volunteers Save America's Youth?* (Philadelphia: Public/Private Ventures, 1997.

11. R. Lubove, *The Struggle for Social Security* (Cambridge: Harvard University Press, 1968), as cited in Salamon and Anheir, "Caring Sector or Caring Society," in

Schervish, Hodgkinson, Gates, and Associates, eds., *Care, Community, and Modern Society*.

12. Julian Wolpert, "Fragmentation in America's Nonprofit Sector," in Schervish, Hodgkinson, Gates, and Associates, eds., *Care, Community, and Modern Society*, pp. 459–77.

13. Michael Briand and Jennifer Alstad, "Strengthening the Democratic Process," in Schervish, Hodgkinson, Gates, and Associates, eds., *Care, Community, and Modern Society*, pp. 313–32.

14. Briand and Alstad, "Strengthening the Democratic Process, p. 326.

15. Freire, *Pedagogy of the Oppressed*, p. 78.

SELECTED BIBLIOGRAPHY

Ainsworth, M. D. S., M. C. Blehar, E. Waters, and S. Wall. *Patterns of Attachment.* Hillsdale, N.J.: Lawrence Erlbaum Associates, 1978.

Ames, Carole and Russell Ames. *Research on Motivation in Education*; vol. 2: *The Classroom Milieu.* New York: Academic Press, 1985.

Anderson, Jim. *Courageous Teaching: Creating a Caring Community in the Classroom.* Thousand Oaks, Calif.: Corwin Press, 1995.

Bellah, Robert N., Richard Madsen, William M. Sullivan, Ann Swidler, and Steven M. Tipton. *Habits of the Heart: Individualism and Commitment in American Life.* Berkeley: University of California Press, 1985.

Benson, Peter L. *The Troubled Journey: A Portrait of 6th–12th Grade Youth.* Minneapolis: Search Institute, 1993.

Bluestein, Jeffrey. *Care and Commitment: Taking the Personal Point of View.* New York: Oxford University Press, 1991.

Bowlby, John. *A Secure Base: Parent-Child Attachment and Healthy Human Development.* New York: Basic Books, 1988.

Brabeck, Mary M., ed. *Who Cares? Theory, Research, and Educational Implications of the Ethic of Care.* New York: Praeger, 1989.

Bubeck, Diemut Elisabet. *Care, Gender, and Justice.* Oxford: Clarendon Press, 1995.

Coleman, James S. *Public and Private High Schools: The Impact of Communities.* New York: Basic Books, 1987.

Coles, Robert. *The Call of Service: A Witness to Idealism.* New York: Houghton Mifflin, 1993.

Edmonds, Janie P. *We Work Harder for Teachers Who Care: Teachers' Caring Behav-

iors as Perceived by Gifted and Challenged Students and Their Teachers. New York: Teachers College Press, 1992.

Eisenberg, Nancy. *The Caring Child*. Cambridge: Harvard University Press, 1992.

Erikson, Eric. *Childhood and Society*. New York: Norton, 1963.

Etzioni, Amitai. *The Spirit of Community: The Reinvention of American Society*. New York: Simon and Schuster, 1993.

Fine, Michelle. *Framing Dropouts: Notes on the Politics of an Urban Public High School*. Albany: State University of New York Press, 1991.

Fogel, Alan and Gail F. Melson, eds. *The Origins of Nurturance: Developmental, Biological, and Cultural Perspectives on Caregiving*. Hillsdale, N.J.: Lawrence Erlbaum, 1986.

Freedman, Marc. *The Kindness of Strangers: Adult Mentors, Urban Youth, and the New Volunteerism*. San Francisco: Josey-Bass, 1993.

Gallatzer-Levy, Robert M. and Bertram J. Cohler. *The Essential Other: A Developmental Psychology of the Self*. New York: Basic Books, 1993.

Gilligan, Carol. *In a Different Voice: Psychological Theory and Women's Development*. Cambridge: Harvard University Press, 1982.

Ianni, Francis A. J. *The Search for Structure: A Report on American Youth Today*. New York: Free Press, 1989.

Kett, Joseph F. *Rites of Passage: Adolescence in America 1790 to the Present*. New York: Basic Books, 1977.

Killen, Melanie and Daniel Hart, eds. *Morality in Everyday Life: Developmental Perspectives*. New York: Cambridge University Press, 1995.

Kramer, R. M. and T. R. Tyler. *Trust in Organizations: Frontiers of Theory and Research*. Thousand Oaks, Calif: Sage, 1996.

Kurtines, William M., Margarita Azmitia, and Jacob L. Gewirtz, eds. *The Role of Values in Psychology and Human Development*. New York: Wiley, 1992.

Larrabee, Mary Jeanne. *An Ethic of Care: Feminist and Interdisciplinary Perspectives*. New York: Routledge, 1993.

Noddings, Nel. *Caring: A Feminine Approach to Ethics and Moral Education*. Berkeley: University of California Press, 1984.

Noddings, Nel. *The Challenge to Care in Schools: An Alternative Approach to Education*. New York: Teachers College Press, 1992.

Oliner, Samuel P. and Pearl M. Oliner. *The Altruistic Personality: Rescuers of Jews in Nazi Europe*. New York: Free Press, 1988.

Shervish, Paul G., Virginia A. Hodgkinson, Margaret Gates, and Associates, eds. *Care and Community in Modern Society: Passing On the Tradition of Service to Future Generations*. San Francisco: Jossey-Bass, 1995.

Sorokin, Pitirim A. *The Ways and Power of Love*. Chicago: Henry Regnery, 1967.

Taylor, Charles. *Sources of the Self: The Making of the Modern Identity.* Cambridge: Harvard University Press, 1989.

Tronto, Joan C. *Moral Boundaries: A Political Argument for an Ethic of Care.* New York: Routledge, 1993.

Werner, Emmy E. and Ruth S. Smith. *Overcoming the Odds: High Risk Children from Birth to Adulthood.* Ithaca: Cornell University Press, 1992.

Whiting, Beatrice Blyth and Carolyn Pope Edwards. *Children of Different Worlds: The Formation of Social Behavior.* Cambridge: Harvard University Press, 1988.

Whiting, Beatrice B. and John W. M. Whiting. *Children of Six Cultures: A Psycho-Cultural Analysis.* Cambridge: Harvard University Press, 1975.

Wuthnow, Robert. *Learning to Care: Elementary Kindness in an Age of Indifference.* New York: Oxford University Press, 1995.

Wuthnow, Robert. *Acts of Compassion: Caring for Others and Helping Ourselves.* Princeton: Princeton University Press, 1991.

Youniss, J. and M. Yates. *Community Service and Social Responsibility in Youth.* Chicago: University of Chicago Press, 1997.

INDEX